Flea Market
Furniture Makeovers

Flea Market Furniture Makeovers

Mickey Baskett

Sterling Publishing Co., Inc.
New York

Prolific Impressions Production Staff:

Editor in Chief: Mickey Baskett
Copy Editor: Phyllis Mueller
Graphics: Dianne Miller, Karen Turpin
Styling: Kirsten Jones
Photography: Jerry Mucklow
Administration: Jim Baskett

Library of Congress Cataloging-in-Publication Data Available

10 9 8 7 6 5 4 3 2 1

Published in paperback in 2006 by Sterling Publishing Co., Inc.
387 Park Avenue South, New York, N.Y. 10016

© 2004 by Prolific Impressions, Inc.

Produced by Prolific Impressions, Inc.
160 South Candler St., Decatur, GA 30030

Distributed in Canada by Sterling Publishing
c/o Canadian Manda Group, 165 Dufferin Street,
Toronto, Ontario, Canada M6K 3H6
Distributed in the United Kingdom by GMC Distribution Services,
Castle Place, 166 High Street, Lewes, East Sussex, England BN7 1XU
Distributed in Australia by Capricorn Link (Australia) Pty. Ltd.
P.O. Box 704, Windsor, NSW 2756 Australia

Printed in China
All rights reserved

Sterling ISBN-13: 978-1-4027-0640-0 Hardcover
        ISBN-10: 1-4027-0640-5

        ISBN-13: 978-1-4027-3462-5 Paperback
        ISBN-10: 1-4027-3462-X

For information about custom editions, special sales, premium and corporate purchases, please contact Sterling Special Sales Department at 800-805-5489 or specialsales@sterlingpub.com.

Acknowledgements

Mickey Baskett thanks the following for their generous contributions:

For supplying artists with painting products such as FolkArt® Acrylic Colors; Durable Colors™ indoor/outdoor paint; FolkArt® varnishes; Apple Barrel® indoor/outdoor acrylic bottle paints; Decorator Products® tools and stamps:
Plaid Enterprises, Inc.
3223 Westech Dr.
Norcross, GA 30092
www.plaidonline.com

For paint brushes:
Silver Brush Ltd.
P.O. Box 414
Windsor, N.J. 08561-0414
Phone 609-443-4900
Fax 609-443-4888
www.silverbrush.com

For primer and varnish:
J.W. Etc. Fine Quality Products
2205 First Street
Suite 103
Simi Valley, CA 95065
Phone 805-526-5066
Fax 905-526-1297
www.jwetc.com

CONTENTS

With paint, you can give new life to old, castoff furniture and transform inexpensive, unfinished pieces—making them into fantastic and fanciful works of art that add a personal touch to the rooms of your home. And what's more, you can

Try Some Furniture Transformations

save lots of money. With today's emphasis on recycling and with America's love affair with all things old and shabby, you can make a $3.00 chair look like a $300.00 chair. With some wonderful paint colors, a design that suites your decorating style, and a few tricks you will learn in this book, you can create decorator pieces for your home — the kind that are sold in furniture boutiques for big bucks.

The projects in this book present an array of techniques for decorating and refurbishing chairs, tables, chests of drawers, cabinets, and accessories. They showcase a range of styles and designs. Some are rustic, some are refined; some are simple, others are sophisticated. The techniques used to create the pieces employ decorative painting, decoupage, crackling, distressing, gold leafing, sponging, staining, stamping,

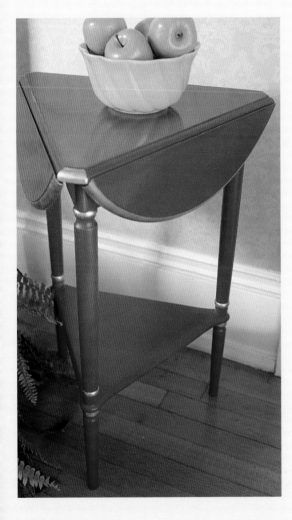

and stenciling. They range in complexity from simple pieces perfect for beginners that include staining, decoupage, and stamping to more advanced projects that include decorative painting and faux finishing techniques. There are step-by-step instructions and numerous photographs to guide you.

Using furniture pieces you decorated yourself is a rewarding and creative way to add personal touches to the rooms of your home and a great way to turn a furniture bargain into a furniture beauty.

FURNITURE PREPARATION

Supplies

▪ For Cleaning & Stripping

Mild Detergent or Bubble Bath:

If you are going to paint your piece of furniture, you will find that stripping it is not necessary—you just need to clean it up. To remove dirt, dust, cobwebs, etc., use a cleaner that does not leave a gritty residue. Effective cleaners include **mild dishwashing detergent** and **bubble bath**. Mix the cleaner with water and wash the furniture with a cellulose sponge. Rinse and wipe dry with soft cloth rags.

Paint Thinner:

Use **paint thinner** and a **steel wool pad** to remove waxy buildup on stained wooden pieces and old varnish. Shellac can be removed with rubbing alcohol.

Paint Stripper:

There are several reasons you may wish to strip a piece of furniture. If you plan to stain, pickle, or color wash the piece, you will need to get down to bare wood. And if the piece of furniture is covered with layers of badly flaking, wrinkled, or uneven paint that can't be sanded smooth, stripping is necessary. There are many brands of paint strippers available at do-it-yourself and hardware stores. Apply **paint stripper** with a brush. When the paint begins to wrinkle and lift, remove it with a **paint scraper.**

▪ For Sanding & Filling

Sandpaper:

Sandpaper is available in different grits for different types of sanding. Generally, start with medium grit sandpaper, and then use fine grit to sand before painting. Between coats of paint, sand lightly with fine or extra fine sandpaper.

Sanding Block:

This wooden block that sandpaper is wrapped around aids smooth sanding on flat surfaces.

Electric Sander:

A handheld **electric finishing sander** aids in sanding large, flat areas. Use wet/dry sandpaper and wet it to keep down dust. Wipe away sanding dust with a **tack cloth.**

Wood Filler:

Wood filler or wood putty, applied with a **putty knife**, is used to fill cracks, holes, dents, and nicks for a smooth, even painting surface. You can use wood filler on raw wood furniture or previously painted or stained furniture. Let dry and sand smooth.

▪ For Priming & Base Painting

Primer:

A **primer** fills and seals wood and helps paint to bond properly. A **stain blocking primer** keeps an old finish from bleeding through new paint. This is especially necessary if you have a dark piece of furniture and want to paint it a light color. Always allow primer to dry thoroughly before base painting.

You can make your own primer by slightly thinning white flat latex wall paint with water. One coat on an old painted or stained piece helps give the surface some "tooth" so the base paint will adhere properly.

Paint for Base Painting:

Base paint is the first layer of paint applied to a surface after a primer. Base paint your furniture piece with **latex wall paint in an eggshell of satin finish, acrylic indoor/outdoor paint,** or **acrylic craft paint**. Brush on the paint, using long, smooth strokes. Work carefully to avoid runs, drips, or sags.

All the painting in this book was done with waterbase paints. Today's formulas provide as much wear-and-tear protection as oil-based paints.

Brushes:

Base paint can be applied with a **foam brush** or **bristle paint brush**. For painting details or smaller areas, use a 1" **craft brush**. For painting larger flat areas, a **foam roller** is a good choice.

Miscellaneous Supplies:

Wear **latex gloves** to protect your hands from cleaners, solvents, and paints. These tight-fitting gloves, available at hardware stores, paint stores, and home improvement centers, will not impair your dexterity.

Masking Tape:

This often under-valued supply is essential for furniture decorating. Use **masking tape** to mask off areas for painting, to make crisp lines, and to protect previously painted areas. ❑

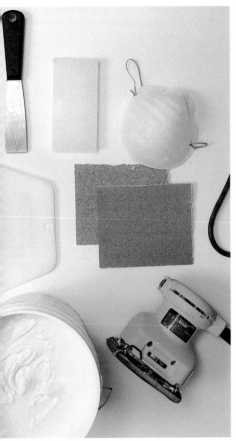

Pictured clockwise from top left: putty knife, sanding block, breathing mask, sandpaper, electric sander, putty, smoothing tool.

Pictured: various primers, sealers, and paints for furniture preparation and base painting.

Old Furniture to Be Painted

Flea markets, tag and yard sales, and used furniture stores are good sources of old furniture for painting. So are those pieces of furniture that have languished for years in your attic, basement, or garage. When selecting an old furniture piece, choose one in sound condition. If the legs are wobbly or the drawers stick, make repairs before painting. Repair loose joints with wood glue. If extensive repairs are needed, seek the services of a professional.

Photo 1 - Removing hardware.

When an old piece of furniture is to receive a painted finish, very often all the piece needs is cleaning and sanding. A primer coat may be necessary if the piece has a glossy finish. If the finish is in very bad condition or the varnish is wrinkled and chipped, you may choose to strip it. Stripping is usually a last resort.

A good rule of thumb is to work with what you have. If your old piece of furniture has a dark finish, perhaps you'll decide to paint it dark green to minimize the amount of preparation you'll need to do, instead of trying to cover up the dark finish with a light paint color.

Study your piece to determine how much preparation needs to be done.

Step 1 - Removing Hardware:

Before cleaning or sanding, remove all hardware, such as door and drawer pulls. (**photo 1**) Depending upon your piece and what you're planning to do, it also may be necessary to remove hinges, doors, drawers, or mirrors. This is also the time to remove upholstered seats from chairs. Door and drawer pulls and knobs should be painted or treated while they are detached.

Photo 2 - Washing a piece with a mild soapy solution.

Photo 3 - Removing wax buildup with a steel wool pad dipped in paint thinner.

PRECAUTIONS & TIPS

- Read product labels carefully and observe all manufacturer's recommendations and cautions.
- **Always** work in a well-ventilated area or outdoors.
- Wear gloves to protect your hands.
- Wear a dust mask or respirator to protect yourself from dust and fumes.
- Use a piece of old or scrap vinyl flooring for a work surface. Vinyl flooring is more protective and more convenient than layers of newspaper or plastic sheeting. Paint or finishes can seep through newspapers, and newspapers always get stuck to your shoes. Plastic sheeting is slippery. Spills can be wiped up quickly from vinyl, and nothing will seep through it to your floor. Small pieces of vinyl can be purchased inexpensively as remnants at floor covering stores and building supply centers.
- Dispose of solvents properly. If in doubt of how to dispose of them, contact your local government for instructions. Do not pour solvents or paint strippers down drains or toilets.

Photo 4 - Sanding a flat surface with sandpaper wrapped around a sanding block.

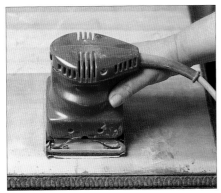

Photo 5 - Sanding a flat surface with a handheld electric finishing sander.

Photo 6 - Sanding in a tight area.

Photo 7 - Filling a crack with wood putty.

Photo 8 - Applying white primer with a bristle paint brush.

SANDING TIPS

• When sanding old paint that may contain lead, use wet/dry sandpaper and wet the paper while sanding to prevent creating dust.

• **Always** wear a mask when sanding to prevent inhaling dust.

Step 2 - Cleaning:

The next step is removing accumulated dust, grease, and grime. Sometimes careful cleaning is all that's needed before painting. To clean, mix a little mild detergent or bubble bath with water in a bucket or basin. Using a household sponge, wash the piece with the soapy solution (**photo 2**). Rinse with clear water. Wipe the piece with soft cloth rags to remove surface water. Allow to air dry until the piece is completely dry.

If your piece has years of wax buildup or is covered with shellac or varnish that has cracked or worn unevenly, use a solvent to provide a thorough cleaning. This is necessary because wax repels waterbase paints, and shellac and varnish are poor undercoats for paint. Pour a solvent such as paint thinner, mineral spirits, or a liquid sandpaper product in a metal can or enamel bowl. Dip a steel wool pad in the solvent and rub the surface (**photo 3**). Rinse the pad in solvent occasionally as you work, and replace the solvent in your container when it gets dirty. When you're finished, allow the piece to air dry.

Step 3 - Sanding:

An important step in the preparation process, sanding dulls the old finish so new paint will adhere properly and creates a smooth surface for painting. To sand the piece smooth, start with medium grit sandpaper, then use fine grit. Always sand in the direction of the grain. Wrap the sandpaper around a sanding block on flat surfaces (**photo 4**). Use a handheld electric finishing sander on larger flat areas, such as tops and shelves (**photo 5**). Hold the paper in your hand when working in tight areas or on curves (**photo 6**). Wipe away dust with a tack cloth. To remove sanding dust from crevices and tight areas, use a brush or a vacuum cleaner.

Step 4 - Filling and Smoothing:

Fill cracks, dents, nicks, and holes with a paste wood filler or wood putty. Apply the paste with a putty knife, smoothing the material as much as possible and removing any excess before it dries. Follow manufacturer's recommendations regarding drying time. If necessary, apply a second time and let dry thoroughly. Sand smooth when dry. Wipe away dust.

Step 5 - Priming or Undercoating:

Priming or undercoating seals the wood and prevents dark areas from showing through a light colored base paint. Don't use a primer if you intend to apply a stain or color wash. And if you're planning to create a distressed finish that involves sanding through layers of paint or that will reveal some bare wood, don't use a primer.

For most finishes, flat white latex wall paint that has been diluted with a little water is an appropriate primer. Mix the paint with a little water (about 10%) to make it go on smoothly.

If your piece has a dark stained or varnished surface, apply a stain blocking white primer so the dark stain or varnish won't bleed through your new paint. Stain blocking primers are also available as sprays.

To make your own stain blocking primer, mix equal amounts of white latex wall paint and acrylic varnish. Sponge this mixture over the surface of your piece.

Allow primer to dry overnight. Sand again, lightly, for a smooth surface. Wipe away dust. You're ready to paint!

Continued on next page

Step 6 - Base Painting:

The base paint is the foundation upon which you build your decorative effects—you can sponge over it, rag it, add decorative painted elements, distress it, or antique it. There are a number of types of paints that will work for base painting. I prefer an eggshell finish or satin finish acrylic or latex paint. Craft shops or hardware stores sell acrylic or latex paints in small amounts that work great for painting furniture. Even wall paint will be fine—as long as it has a satin finish rather than a flat finish. Indoor/outdoor paint with a matte or satin finish is also a wonderful base paint.

Because it is your foundation, you want the base paint to be smooth and to have thoroughly covered the old paint or finish. Apply base paint with a small roller or a wide fine-bristled brush. Apply one light coat and allow it to dry. Sand with fine sandpaper to smooth the surface. Apply a second coat and allow it to dry thoroughly. If any of the old finish still shows, apply a third coat. Allow to dry. You are now ready to enjoy your piece or to add additional decorative effects.

Optional Stripping

Furniture that was previously painted doesn't need stripping if the finish is sound and not too thick. However, if the existing paint or varnish is chipped, blistered, or cracked, or if the original finish was poorly applied, or if the paint on the piece is so thick it's obscuring the lines or details of the piece, stripping is warranted. You can, of course, have the stripping done by a professional—all you'll need to do is sand the piece afterward. Sometimes it costs less to have a professional do the job than it would to buy the supplies and equipment to do the job yourself.

If you wish to strip the piece yourself, purchase a liquid, gel, or paste product specifically made for the job you're doing. (These generally are labeled "stripper" or "paint remover" and may be waterbased or solvent-based.) Read the label carefully and follow the instructions exactly. Work in a well-ventilated space and wear gloves, goggles, and protective clothing.

Step 1 - Applying the Stripper:

Apply an even layer of stripper to the surface with a bristle brush (**photo 10**) in the direction of the grain of the wood. Wait the recommended amount of time. The old paint or finish will soften, look wrinkled, and start to lift. Be patient! Chemical strippers give the best results when you allow them enough time to work properly.

Step 2 - Removing the Old Finish:

Use a paint scraper to lift the old finish from the surface (**photo 11**), again working in the direction of the grain. Be careful not to gouge or scrape the surface as you work. On curves, in crevices, and on carved areas, remove the old finish with steel wool, an old bristle brush, toothpicks, or rags.

Finishing Your Project

When all your decorating is complete, you need to protect the surface. If you haven't used indoor/outdoor paint for base painting and decorating, you will want to give your finished piece a protective coating. Use waterbase varnishes and sealers that are compatible with acrylic paints for sealing and finishing. They are available in brush on and spray formulations. Choose products that are non-yellowing and quick drying.

Varnishes and sealers are available in a variety of finishes—matte, satin, and gloss. Satin is my favorite. It gives a nice luster but doesn't emphasize uneven brush strokes like a gloss finish can.

Apply the finish according to the manufacturer's instructions. Several thin coats are better than one thick coat. Let dry between coats according to the manufacturer's recommendations. A furniture piece such as a breakfast table, which will receive a lot of use, will need more coats of sealer or varnish for protection than a piece that is decorative or receives less use.

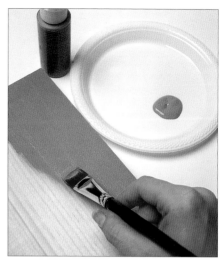

Photo 9 - Base painting after priming.

Photo 10 - Applying the stripper with a bristle brush.

Photo 11 - Lifting the softened old finish with a paint scraper.

New Unfinished Wood Furniture

Although this book emphasizes the use of flea market finds — you can create the same look with unfinished furniture pieces. New unfinished wood furniture requires less preparation than old furniture—often sanding and priming are all that's necessary.

Step 1 - Sanding:

Sand the furniture with fine grit sandpaper, sanding with the grain of the wood, to remove rough edges and smooth the surface. Use a sanding block (**photo 1**) or handheld electric sander on flat surfaces. Hold the paper in your hand on curved areas. Remove dust with a tack cloth or a dry dust cloth. Don't use a damp cloth—the dampness could raise the grain of the wood.

On some furniture, glue may have seeped out of the joints. It's important to remove any glue residue—paint won't adhere to it. If possible, sand away the dried glue. If sanding doesn't remove it, scrape it lightly with a craft knife.

Step 2 - Sealing (Optional):

If there are knots or dark places on the piece, seal them with clear sealer or shellac (**photo 2**). Let dry completely. This will keep sap or residue from bleeding through the base paint.

Step 3 - Filling (Optional):

If your piece has nail holes, gaps, or cracks, fill them with wood filler or wood putty, using a putty knife. Smooth the material as much as possible and remove any excess before it dries. Follow manufacturer's recommendations regarding drying time. When dry, sand smooth. Wipe away dust.

Step 4 - Priming:

Paint the piece with a coat of diluted flat white latex wall paint (mixed by adding about 10% water to paint) or spray primer (**photo 3**). Let dry thoroughly. Sand with fine sandpaper. Wipe away dust with a tack cloth.

Step 5 - Base Painting:

The base paint is the foundation upon which you build your decorative effects—you can sponge over it, rag it, add decorative painted elements, distress it, or antique it. Because it is your foundation, you want it to be smooth and to have thoroughly covered the wood. Apply base paint with a small roller or a wide fine-bristled brush. Apply one light coat and allow it to dry. Sand with fine sandpaper to smooth the surface. Apply a second coat and allow it to dry thoroughly. You are now ready to enjoy your piece or to add additional decorative effects.

Photo 1 - Sanding with a sanding block.

Photo 2 - Sealing with shellac.

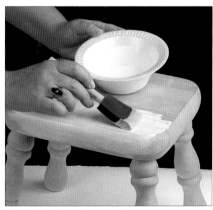

Photo 3 - Applying a primer.

DECORATING TECHNIQUES

Decorative Painting

Painted designs are a wonderful way to create a decorative focal point for a room or a coordinated, custom look on furniture. Just looking through the pages of this book will show you how versatile painted designs can be. I think every room should have at least one piece of painted furniture in it. It adds a personal style statement to your room.

BASIC SUPPLIES

■ Paints

Acrylic craft paints, sold in 2 oz. bottles, were used to paint the designs. There are a variety of brands of these acrylic craft paints that are formulated especially for decorative painting or design painting. They are thicker and more opaque with pigment than most acrylic paints. They come in a wide array of pre-mixed colors and are available a craft shops or departments. They are inexpensive to buy and easy to use, even for beginners. Cleanup is easy with soap and water.

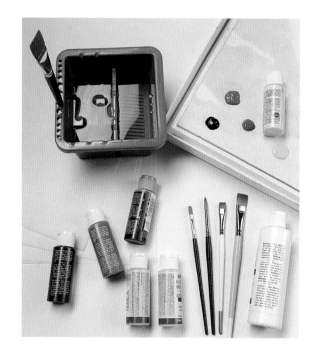

■ Brushes

You'll need an assortment of artist's paint brushes—rounds, liners, and flats in various sizes—for decorative painting. Use round or flat brushes for applying color, flat brushes for blending, shading and highlighting, and liner brushes for painting details and outlining. You will find these in art stores or in art or decorative painting departments of craft shops.

■ Palette

For loading your brushes, you'll need a palette or a disposable foam plate. A "stay-wet" palette is best to use when painting with acrylic paints. This type of palette has a wet sponge under a piece of wax coated paper. This keeps the paints moist and ready to use.

■ Water container

A water container is needed for rinsing brushes.

■ Pattern Transferring Supplies

Patterns are included for all the designs. You can paint your design free-hand by using the pattern as a guide, or you can transfer the pattern directly to your furniture piece. Use **tracing paper** and a **pencil** to trace the design from the book. Then you can enlarge or reduce the pattern as needed to fit your surface. Use **transfer paper** and a **stylus** to transfer the design to the surface.

Steps to Successful Decorative Painting

1. Prepare the Furniture
Prepare the furniture piece according to the instructions in the "Preparation" section.

2. Trace & Transfer Pattern
Trace pattern from book on tracing paper. Enlarge or reduce pattern to fit, if needed. Transfer design to surface, using transfer paper and a stylus (**photo 1, photo 2**).

3. Prepare Palette
Squeeze puddles of paint on a palette or disposable foam plate. Leave space

Photo 1. Transferring design to surface.

Photo 2. Lifting the transfer paper reveals the transferred design, ready for painting.

Photo 3. A "stay-wet" palette with puddles of paint.

Photo 4 - Basecoating the design area.

Photo 5 - Floating shading on a design.

Photo 6 - Floating highlights on a design.

on the palette for loading brushes and blending colors. A "stay-wet" palette will keep your paints moist and ready for painting. (**photo 3**)

4. Paint the Design

You can paint the designs shown using a very simple technique I call "colorbook painting," which is merely painting the areas of the design one color. Then, using black paint or a permanent marker, outline the design. Or, you can use a decorative painting technique where areas of the design are shaded and highlighted.

• **Basecoat the design area.**
The basecoat is the first layer of paint that a part of a design receives. For example, if you are painting a flower and leaf design, you would first fill in the entire leaf with a green color as specified. A good rule of thumb is to use the largest brush you can handle

that fits the area of the design you're painting. (**photo 4**)

• **Float the shading on the design.**
Shading creates shadows, darkens and deepens color, and makes an area recede. In decorative painting, one side of a painted subject is often shaded to add depth and dimension. To "float" the shading, load the brush with a floating medium or a little water. Load brush with the green color that is the predominant color of the design (for example: the green basecoat color of the leaf). Then pull one side of the brush through a darker shade of color to load just the side of the brush. Stroke the brush back and forth on the palette to blend the colors. Apply this to the design, with the dark side of the brush on the outside, or dark side, of the design. (**photo 5**)

• **Float the highlighting on the design.**
Highlighting creates dimension by adding light in the form of a lighter color and makes an area seem closer. This technique is done in the same way as floating shading—load the brush with the predominant color, then sideload the brush with a lighter shade. (**photo 6**)

• **Add details.**
Details are painted last. The amount of detail depends on the particular design. Most often, this refers to using a thin liner brush loaded with black paint to add definition to the design.

Optional - Outlining: Outlining, adding a dark line around the edge of a design for emphasis, is usually done with a liner brush. Outlining also may be done with a fine tip permanent marker.

Crackling

The age and character that naturally comes from years of wind and weather can be easily created on painted surfaces with crackle medium.

Two-color crackle uses two latex paint colors—one for the basecoat and one for the topcoat. The crackle medium is applied between the coats of paint, causing the topcoat to crack and reveal the basecoat.

A variation of this method would be to apply varnish over the crackle medium instead of the second paint color. When varnish dries, rub antiquing into the cracks.

BASIC SUPPLIES

◾ Paint

Use latex wall paint in an eggshell or satin (not flat) finish for larger projects or acrylic craft paint for smaller projects. You'll need one paint color for the basecoat in the one-color method and two colors (one basecoat, one topcoat) for the two-color method.

◾ Crackle Medium

Crackle medium is a clear liquid. It does not crack, but any waterbase medium (paint or varnish, or example) applied on top of it reacts by shrinking and forming cracks, creating the distinctive crackled look.

◾ Brushes

Use **foam brushes** to apply paint and crackle medium. Use a **sponge** to rub antiquing medium or tinted glaze into the cracks for the one-color method.

◾ Varnish

For the protection, apply a brush-on clear waterbase varnish over the project.

HERE'S HOW

Two-Color Crackle

1. Apply the first paint color. Let dry.

2. Apply crackle medium. Let dry.

3. Apply second paint color. Cracks will form as the paint dries.

Variation: Use varnish applied over crackle medium instead of second paint color. Rub antiquing into cracks that have formed.

◾ Antiquing

For the variation method, rub an antiquing medium or tinted glaze (neutral glazing medium + color) into the cracks in the varnish.

Distressing

Distressed finishes add the character imparted by use and age. You can create a simple distressed finish by painting a piece with layers of color and sanding or scraping the piece after the paint has dried. This removes some of the paint, exposing layers of color and allowing some of the wood to show. **Don't** use a primer if you're planning to distress a piece and sand down to the wood.

SANDING TIPS

- Sand more on the edges of the piece — concentrating your efforts in places where wear would normally occur over time — and less on flat areas for a more natural appearance.
- Don't use a sanding block or an electric sander — you want an uneven look. Holding the sandpaper in your hand is best and allows you more control.
- Use medium or medium-fine grit sandpaper to remove more paint, fine grit sandpaper to remove less.
- It's best to begin slowly and err on the side of removing too little paint rather than too much. You can always sand again to remove more. Stop when the result pleases you.

BASIC SUPPLIES

■ Paint
You'll need two (or more) colors of latex or acrylic paint to create the layers of color.

■ Sandpaper
Use sandpaper to remove paint and reveal the layers. You'll need medium, medium-fine, and fine grit sandpapers.

■ Wax stick
Applying wax to the surface between coats of paint makes the succeeding coats easier to remove. You can buy a wax stick for this purpose from a crafts store or use a piece of a candle or a paraffin block.

■ Metal scraper
A metal scraper or putty knife can be used to remove paint from the surface and to create dings and dents characteristic of wear and age.

■ Brushes
Use foam brushes or flat bristle brushes for applying the layers of paint.

■ Tack cloth
Use a tack cloth to wipe away sanding dust.

HERE'S HOW

1. Paint piece with first paint color. Let dry.

3. Paint with second paint color. Let dry.

2. Apply wax to areas of piece where wear would normally occur.

4. Sand and/or scrape paint to reveal paint layers and/or bare wood. After sanding, use a tack cloth to wipe away dust. ❑

Gold Leafing

Gold leafing is an elegant, traditional way to add a warm metallic glow to surfaces. Once you try it and see how easy it is to add luxurious beauty to a piece, you will be hooked. Metal leafing sheets and leaf adhesive are easy to use and available at art supply and crafts stores.

BASIC SUPPLIES

■ Acrylic paint

Use a dark color acrylic paint as a base paint for gold leafing if you are planning to apply leaf to an entire surface. A dark red paint adds a rich base and gives depth to the metal leafing.

■ Metal leafing

Metal leaf sheets are very thin squares of metal (real gold or imitation) that are applied to a surface. Metal leafing is also available in silver, copper, and variegated colors.

■ Leaf adhesive

Leaf adhesive holds the leaf to the surface. Follow the adhesive manufacturer's instructions regarding drying times. The adhesive should be slightly tacky to the touch when the leafing is applied.

■ Pencil with eraser

Use a pencil with a new, flat eraser to lift sheets of leafing.

HERE'S HOW

1. Paint area to be leafed with dark red paint. Let dry.

2. Brush leaf adhesive over the area and let dry, following manufacturer's instructions.

3. Apply sheets of leafing to cover adhesive, one sheet at a time. To pick up leafing sheets, use the eraser end of a pencil after moistening the eraser by touching it to a damp (not wet) cloth. (It is almost like floating the leafing onto the surface.) Lightly press the leafing on the surface, using the soft brush. Repeat, overlapping the pieces, until the surface is covered. Wrinkles are okay—they can be patted flat, and they add charm. It is also okay to have some areas where the paint shows—this adds a beautifully worn look.

4. Pounce the surface lightly with a soft brush to smooth. Brush away bits of the leaf. Rub the piece with a very soft cloth, such as a piece of velvet, to further smooth it.

Optional Antiquing: If the gold looks too garish for you or if your piece has a lot of dimension and carved areas, you may want to add antiquing. Here's how: Working one small area at a time, brush antiquing on the piece. Use a soft cloth to wipe off excess antiquing (how much is "excess" is up to you). Continue until you have antiqued the entire piece.

■ Brushes

Use a foam brush for base painting and for applying leaf adhesive. Use a very soft bristle brush to smooth the leafed surface and brush away crumbs of leafing. (A make-up brush is perfect for this, or use a 3/4" or #12 flat artist's brush.)

Sponging

Sponging—creating a texture or pattern on a surface with a sponge—can be done randomly for a textured look or with sponge shapes to create a pattern. Variations in the sponge's surface create variations in the effect.

◼ Sponges

Natural sea sponges are most often used for textures; cellulose kitchen sponges can be easily cut with scissors to make shapes for sponged patterns. You can also tear the edges of a cellulose sponge to create an irregular shape that can be used for sponging textures. Both types of sponges may be purchased attached to mitts. Find them at hardware and crafts stores.

◼ Paint

Use latex paint (for larger areas) or acrylic craft paint (for smaller projects.) You'll need two (or more) colors. To create transparent sponged effects, mix the paint you're using for sponging with an equal amount of neutral glazing medium.

◼ Tray or plates

Pouring paint for sponging on a paint tray or a disposable foam or plastic plate makes it easier to load the sponge.

HERE'S HOW

1. Base paint the surface. Let dry.
2. Dampen sponge. Squeeze out excess water. Blot sponge on a towel. The sponge should be damp and pliable, but not wet.
3. Pour paint for sponging on a plate or into a paint tray. Press sponge into paint to load. Blot the loaded sponge on a clean disposable plate or a clean part of the paint tray to distribute the paint.
4. Pounce the sponge on the surface,

SPONGING TIPS

- To make crisp impressions, don't rub or drag the sponge.
- To keep sponging from getting too dense, don't overwork the surface—pounce and move on.
- To avoid a repeated texture, change the position of your hand so the sponge isn't in the same position every time you touch the surface.
- Be sure some of the background color shows through.

slightly overlapping each application to create texture.

Staining

Staining imparts vibrant hues to wood while allowing the grain and natural characteristics of the wood to show through. The technique can be used to create designs or to create backgrounds for stained, stenciled, stamped, or painted designs. You can also use stain to mellow the look of a painted design by applying it over the design. Simply brush on the stain and wipe away the excess—that's it.

BASIC SUPPLIES

◼ Stain

Stains are available in a wide variety of pre-mixed wood tones and colors, and it's easy to create custom colors by mixing neutral glazing medium with paint. *Options:*

- Acrylic stain, available in a variety of pre-mixed shades (wood tones and colors).
- Oil-based stain, available in a variety of pre-mixed shades (wood tones and colors).

- Acrylic paint, latex paint, or paint glaze mixed with neutral glazing medium. The proportion of paint to glazing medium is a matter of personal preference. If you want a more transparent stain, use more glazing medium than paint. (Try two parts glazing medium to one part paint.) If you want a more opaque stain, use more paint and less glazing medium. You can buy neutral glazing medium at stores that sell faux finishing supplies.

◼ Brushes

Use a sponge, a sponge brush, or a bristle brush to apply stain.

◼ Rags

Use soft, lint-free cloth rags to wipe away excess stain and buff surfaces.

Stenciling

Stenciling is a centuries-old decorative technique for adding painted designs to surfaces in which paint is applied through the cutout areas of a paint-resistant material.

BASIC SUPPLIES

Stencils

Stencils are available at crafts and home improvement stores in a huge array of pre-cut designs. You can also buy stencil blank material and cut your own stencils with a craft knife.

Paints

A variety of paints can be used for stenciling, including acrylic craft paint, spray paint, stencil gels (gel-like paints that produce a transparent, watercolor look), and cream stencil paints.

Applicators

The paints can be applied with stencil brushes, small paint rollers, or sponge-on-a-stick applicators (round foam sponges on handles). It's good to have several sizes of brushes—the size of the brush to use is determined by the size of the stencil opening.

Palette

Squeeze puddles of paint on a palette or a disposable foam or plastic plate for loading brushes and applicators.

HERE'S HOW

1. Pour some paint on a plate or palette. Holding the stencil brush perpendicular to the plate, dip the tips of the bristles in paint.

2. Lightly pounce the brush on a paper towel to remove excess paint.

3. Apply the paint by pouncing the brush up and down in the openings of the stencil or by moving the brush in a circular motion (this is known as the sweeping stroke), using more pressure to create a darker print. ❑

Decoupage

Decoupage—the art of applying paper or fabric to surfaces and covering the surface with a finish—can add texture, color, and designs to surfaces. You can use the decoupage technique to completely cover a surface or add spot motifs with cutouts.

BASIC SUPPLIES

▧ Decoupage Medium

Traditionally, decoupage was done with glue and layers of varnish. Today's decoupage medium is a clear-drying liquid that is used as both glue and finish. You can find decoupage finish in most craft shops or craft departments.

▧ Paper

Gift wrap, art prints, calendars, photocopies of your photographs, and pages from books of clip art (find them at art supply stores) can all be used. You'll also find papers made especially for decoupaging at crafts stores. Fabric and fabric cutouts can also be used for decoupage. Since most of today's decoupage finishes are waterbased, you should not have any problem with the printing ink bleeding. (If you are not sure, lightly spray the printed design with a sealer and let dry before cutting.)

▧ Cutting Tools

A pair of good quality, small, sharp scissors are essential for success in cutting out designs. A craft knife with a sharp #11 blade and a self-healing mat are useful for cutting interior areas of motifs and large pieces of paper.

▧ Brushes

Use a foam brush or a very fine-bristle varnish brush to apply decoupage medium.

Pictured clockwise from top left: Acrylic craft paint for base painting; decoupage finish; gift wrap and greeting cards; scissors; palette and foam brush.

HERE'S HOW

1. Cut out motifs from paper or fabric with small scissors.

2. *Either* apply decoupage medium to the backs of cutout motifs with an applicator brush and position on the surface *or* brush decoupage medium on the surface and position paper pieces. Let dry.

3. Apply at least two coats of decoupage medium over the paper or fabric to finish. Let dry between coats.

ROOSTER CABINET

DECORATIVE PAINTING, CRACKLING

The rooster painted on this rustic cabinet belongs to Chris's daughter Jennifer. His name is Fred, and he is quite feisty! Chris says he entertains himself by chasing her granddaughter Deven around the yard.

Chris painted a tromphe l'oeil napkin peeking over the edge of the drawer for a whimsical touch. The backsplash contains tiles that were there when Chris found this piece.

By Chris Stokes

SUPPLIES

Project Surface:
Wooden cabinet with panel door

Latex paint:
Satin finish for base painting piece
  Barnyard Red
  Sunflower

Acrylic craft paint:
For decorative painting the design
  Apple Spice
  Asphaltum
  Burnt Sienna
  Burnt Umber
  Green Forest
  Ivory Black
  Prussian Blue
  Red Light
  Sunflower
  Tapioca
  Yellow Ochre

Mediums and Finishes:
Crackle medium
Waterbase varnish, matte sheen
Oil paint for antiquing - Asphaltum or Burnt Umber

Paint Brushes:
Rake or comb - 1/2"
Liner
Flat shaders - #8, #10
Old toothbrush (for spattering)

Tools & Other Supplies:
Sandpaper
Tack cloth
Clean rag (Chris used an old athletic sock.)
Tracing paper and pencil
Transfer paper and stylus

Photo 1 - Highlighting comb and wattle with Yellow Ochre.

INSTRUCTIONS

Prepare & Base Paint

1. Remove door and drawer pulls. Sand cabinet. Wipe with a tack cloth.
2. Paint entire piece with Barnyard Red. Let dry.
3. Sand paint off edges for a worn look. Wipe away dust.
4. Brush crackle medium over the door panel, following the manufacturer's instructions. Let dry.
5. Paint panel with Sunflower, working quickly. Cracks will appear immediately; do not overstroke—this will remove the effect. Let dry.

Photo 2 - Shading the comb and wattle.

Continued on page 25

Photo 3 - Stroking feathers on the body.

Photo 4 - Painting the darker feathers on the lower body.

continued from page 22

6. Paint drawer pulls with Tapioca.
7. Trace and transfer the design.

Paint the Design

Rooster's Comb & Wattle:
1. Using a #8 flat shader, basecoat comb and wattle with Apple Spice.
2. Using same "dirty brush" that you used for basecoating, touch side of brush into Yellow Ochre. Highlight comb and wattle, keeping light color on the left. (**photo 1**)
3. Using same "dirty brush," load one side of brush with Brunt Sienna. Shade comb and wattle keeping dark side of brush on right. (**photo 2**)
4. Repeat this same technique of shading using Burnt Umber.
5. Deepen shading with Ivory Black.

Rooster's Beak & Legs:
1. Paint with Yellow Ochre.
2. Shade with Burnt Sienna.
3. Deepen shading with Burnt Umber + touch of Ivory Black.
4. Highlight with Yellow Ochre + a touch of Tapioca.

Rooster's Eye:
1. Basecoat with Yellow Ochre.
2. Shade with Burnt Sienna.
3. Paint pupil with Ivory Black.
4. Outline eye with Ivory Black.

Rooster's Feathers:
1. Undercoat head and light feather areas with Yellow Ochre + a little Asphaltum + enough water to make the mixture the consistency of ink. *Note, this is not shown in photo example because we wanted to show the feather strokes in a more contrasting look.*

Continued on next page

Photo 5 - Painting the tail feathers.

Photo 6 - Highlighting the tail feathers.

Photo 7 - Beginning antiquing by loading the sock with paint.

Photo 8 - Rubbing paint around the edges of the panel to shade.

continued from page 25

2. Load 1/2" rake brush with Asphaltum. Then pounce brush into Yellow Ochre. Pull strokes from top of rooster down sides to create feather strokes. (**photo 3**)
3. Pick up Tapioca and Sunflower on the same dirty brush — do not clean it. Highlight light feather areas.
4. Wipe same 1/2" rake brush on a paper towel. Pick up Burnt Umber + Ivory Black and paint the darker bottom and chest areas and the tail feathers by pulling strokes down rooster. (**photo 4**)
5. Load 1/2" rake brush with Green Forest. Then pick up Prussian Blue and Ivory Black. Paint in some darker tail feathers. (**photo 5**)
6. Pull in some highlight strokes on the tail by loading the brush with Green Forest + Prussian Blue + a touch of Tapioca. (**photo 6**)
7. Wipe brush. Load with Tapioca and pull in some light feathers as shown in finished painting.

Grass:
1. Using the rake brush with inky Asphaltum, shade under the rooster.
2. Pick up Green Forest + a touch of Ivory Black and pull up grass blades.
3. Use a liner brush with inky greens, Ivory Black, and Yellow Ochre + a touch of Tapioca to pull wispy grasses.

Napkin:
1. Using the photo as a guide, sketch the napkin on the drawer.
2. Basecoat with Tapioca.
3. Shade underneath (around the edges) with Asphaltum.
4. Paint border stripes with Green Forest and Apple Spice. Let dry.

Photo 9 - Using a lighter touch toward the center of the panel.

Photo 10 - Spattering, using an old toothbrush.

Antiquing & Finishing

1. Put the sock on your hand and, using it like a mitt. Rub it into Asphaltum or Burnt Umber oil paint. (**photo 7**)

2. Rub this paint onto the edges of the panel to shade. (**photo 8**) Use less color as you move to the center of the panel. Oil paint stays workable so you can keep rubbing and/or adding paint until you get the look you like. **photo 9**

3. Rub some oil paint on the door and drawer pulls for an antique look.

4. Let dry. Oil paint may take several days to dry.

5. Load a toothbrush with inky Burnt Umber. Spatter the panel. (**photo 10**) Let dry.

6. Re-install door and drawer pulls.

7. Apply two coats waterbase varnish. Let dry between coats. ❑

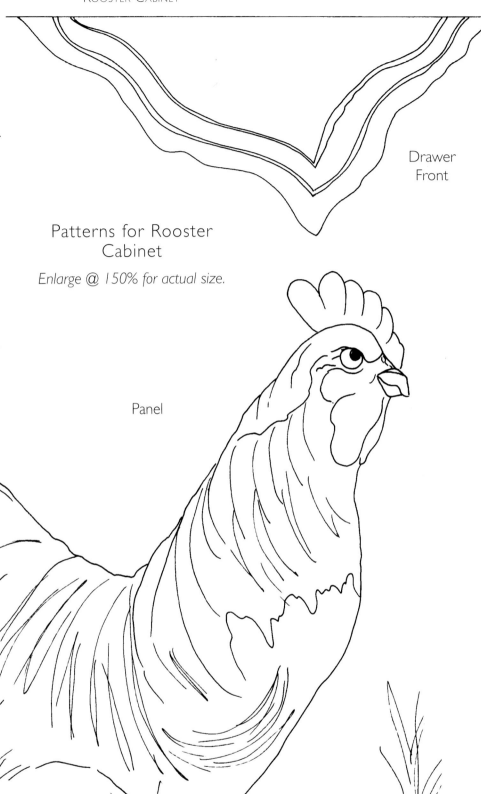

Drawer Front

Patterns for Rooster Cabinet

Enlarge @ 150% for actual size.

Panel

27

FERN FOREST CHEST

DISTRESSING, STENCILING, WOODGRAINING

A nondescript chest gets an exciting decorator look –
a distressed painted finish, stenciled ferns, and a faux woodgrain
top. New twig-motif drawer pulls that are given a rusty
finish complete the transformation.

By Kathi Malarchuk Bailey

The top of the chest has a faux wood-grained finish. Instructions begin on page 30.

FERN FOREST CHEST

SUPPLIES

Project Surface:

Wooden chest of drawers

Latex paint:

Satin finish for base painting piece

    Black

    Creamy Tan

    Rust

Acrylic craft paint:

For stenciling the design

    Cumin

    Light Green

    Medium Green

Mediums & Finishes:

Neutral glazing medium

Waterbase polyurethane varnish, matte or satin sheen

Tools & Brushes:

Fern stencil

Twig-style drawer pulls (These were painted black.)

Wood graining tool

Foam brushes

Foam roller

Wax stick

Stencil brushes

Flat stiff bristle brush (French brush)

Wood putty

Putty knife

Optional: Electric sander

Other Supplies:

Black twig-motif drawer pulls (enough for all the drawers)

Disposable plates

Masking tape

Sandpaper, 80 grit and 220 grit

Tack cloth

INSTRUCTIONS

Prepare

1. Remove drawer pulls and drawers from chest.
2. Sand entire chest, drawer fronts, and top with 80 grit sandpaper to remove old finish and paint. Wipe away dust.
3. Fill holes with wood putty. Allow to dry.
4. Sand with 220 grit paper to smooth. Wipe away dust.
5. Apply masking tape to edges of top so that you won't get paint on it while completing the bottom part of chest.

Photo 1 - Rubbing the wax stick on areas to be distressed.

Photo 2 - Painting with Black latex.

Photo 3 - Sanding with 80 grit sandpaper to remove some of the Black paint.

Photo 4 - Preparing the stencil by taping off adjacent motifs.

Photo 5 - Stenciling a fern with Light Green.

Photo 6 - Deepening the fern color by stenciling areas with Medium Green.

Paint & Distress

1. Basecoat chest base and drawer fronts with two to three coats Rust latex paint. Let dry thoroughly overnight.
2. Rub wax stick at areas where wear would naturally take place—corners, edges, bottoms and parts of the sides are good areas. (**photo 1**) Use the photo as a guide.
3. Paint the entire base with two coats of Black latex paint. (**photo 2**) Let dry between coats. Let second coat dry thoroughly.
4. Use 80 grit paper to remove black paint layer from waxed areas. (**photo 3**)
5. Finish sanding with 220 grit to smooth.

Stencil

1. Prepare the stencil by taping off any other designs that are close to the fern you are going to stencil. (**photo 4**) (The wall border stencil we used had the fern designs positioned close together; taping off the designs on each side of the motifs we're using ensured we would not get unwanted paint on the surface.)
2. Replace drawers in chest.
3. Stencil ferns with Light Green (**photo 5**).
4. Wipe brush. Load into Medium Green and deepen shading on areas of fern. (**photo 6**)

Continued on next page

Photo 7 - The stenciled fern.

Photo 8 - Mixing Cumin paint with glazing medium.

Photo 9 - Rolling the glaze mixture over the top.

Photo 10 - Using the wood graining tool to create the wood grain.

Photo 11 - Dragging the bristle brush over the top to soften the graining.

Continued from page 31

5. Continue stenciling fern onto chest, scattering them over the front and sides and overlapping ferns from drawer to drawer and onto the sides from the front. See closeup of finished fern shown in **photo 7**. Let dry. Remove masking tape from top.

Create Wood Grain on Top

1. Apply masking tape to area of chest that is directly under the top lip so as not to get paint on finished chest.
2. Base paint top with two to three coats Creamy Tan latex paint. Let dry.
3. Mix 3 parts glazing medium with 1 part Cumin paint. (**photo 8**)
4. Use a roller to apply the glaze mixture to the entire top of the chest. *Note:* Glaze dries quickly and cannot be worked after it dries. If the top of your chest is larger than 2 ft. square, section off areas with masking tape for glazing.
5. While the glaze is still wet, rock and drag the wood graining tool across the surface in horizontal strips, over-lapping slightly. (**photo 9**) Wipe off the tool after each drag with a damp rag. Repeat until entire surface is grained.

6. While wood grained glaze is still wet, pull the stiff bristle brush lightly across surface in the same direction as the graining to soften edges and create additional grain. (**photo 11**) Allow to cure 48 hours before sealing.

Finish

1. Lightly pounce black drawer pulls with rust latex paint to simulate rust. Let dry.

2. Apply two to three coats of varnish to chest top, base, drawer fronts, and drawer pulls. Let dry and sand with 220 grit paper between coats. Let final coat dry completely.

3. Attach drawer pulls to drawers. ❏

DIAMONDS BOOKCASE

SPONGING, STENCILING, & STAINING

An ordinary two-shelf bookcase is transformed with sponged diamonds, stenciled flower accents, and stained wood trim. Who doesn't have an old bookcase around that could be transformed.

By Kathi Malarchuk Bailey

SUPPLIES

Project Surface:

Two-shelf bookcase

Latex paint:

Satin finish for base painting
    Butterscotch
    Creamy yellow

Acrylic craft paint:

For stenciling
    Brown-red
    Green
    White

Mediums & Finishes:

White primer
Neutral glazing medium
Wood stain - Dark brown

Tools & Brushes:

Stencil with small flower and leaf
    motifs
Foam roller
Foam brushes
Cellulose sponge
Disposable plates
Small stencil brushes
Pencil
Ruler or tape measure
Hammer
Saw and miter box (for cutting wood
    trim)
Optional: Electric sander

Before

Other Supplies:

Wood trim, width to cover edges and
    enough to cover front edges, top,
    and side edges
Finishing nails
Sandpaper, 80 grit
Tack cloth
Masking tape
Rags

INSTRUCTIONS

Prepare

1. Remove shelf and shelf brackets.
2. Sand top, sides, shelf, and inside of bookcase. Remove dust with tack cloth.

3. Apply two coats of primer to entire bookcase and shelf. Let dry between coats. *My bookcase was a white laminate bookcase so I needed to coat it with a primer to make sure the decorative painting stayed on. This step is optional if using a wooden piece of furniture.*

4. Base paint all pieces with two coats Creamy Yellow latex paint, using the roller for a smooth finish on large areas. Let dry overnight.

Cut, Stain & Attach Trim

1. Measure and cut trim to fit around front, top, bottom ledge, and shelf front and to box in sides – use the photo as a guide for placement. Miter the corners.
2. Apply dark brown wood stain to trim, using a foam brush. Wipe each piece with a stain-dampened rag to remove excess stain. Let dry.
3. Attach trim edges with finishing nails.

Measure & Mark the Diamonds

1. Measure each outer surface panel (top, sides, and shelf). To determine the size and placement of the diamonds, measure and mark the centers of the length and width of each side of each panel with a pencil.

Continued on page 36

continued from page 34

2. Divide the half-length by 3 or 4 (the larger the number, the smaller and more diamonds you will have). Mark the measurements on both sides along the length with a pencil.

Example: If your panel is 24" long, your halfway mark is at 12". Divided by 3, your additional marks are at 3", 6", 9", 12" (the center), 15", 18", and 21".

3. Using a ruler and starting at the top center mark, draw a light diagonal pencil line. Repeat from the bottom center up. Continue this process for each mark, drawing a left and right diagonal line from the top to the bottom and again from bottom to top. When you're finished, you will have a grid of equal-size diamonds. (**photo 1**)

4. On the inside of the bookcase, measure and mark centers of the top and bottom widths and the lengths of both sides. Draw light pencil lines from the top center point to the right and left side centers. Repeat from bottom up to side centers to make a large diamond in center. Repeat on sides and bottom to make half-diamonds.

Sponge Diamonds

1. Mask off individual alternating diamonds. (**photo 2**)

2. Mix 1 part Butterscotch latex paint with 3 parts glazing medium. Dampen sponge with water and squeeze dry.

3. Fill sponge with glaze mixture and pounce inside each masked off diamond. (**photo 3**) Let dry. Remove all masking tape.

4. Mask off alternating diamonds (**photo 4**) and pounce inside them with the glaze mixture, using the sponge. (**photo 5**) Let dry. Remove tape.

5. Mask off stained wood trim so you won't get paint on it from the next steps.

6. Mix 1 part Butterscotch paint with 6 parts glazing medium. (This is a lighter tint.) (**photo 6**) Dampen roller.

7. Dip roller in glaze mixture. Roll over all unglazed diamonds on the outside and the background on the inside. (**photo 7**) Let dry overnight.

Stencil

1. Stencil small white flowers where diamonds intersect on the top, the shelf top, and along the bottom with White paint, using a stencil brush.

2. Stencil stems and leaves with Green paint and clusters of five flowers with White paint at the centers of the diamonds on each side panel, using a stencil brush.

3. Add Red centers to all white flowers, dipping the handle end of a stencil brush in paint. Let dry overnight.

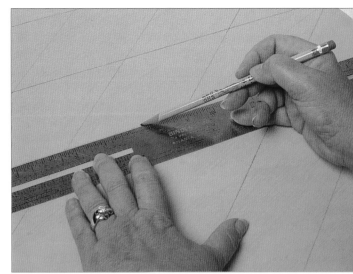

Photo 1 - Drawing lines for the diamonds.

Photo 2 - Masking off diamonds.

Photo 3 - Sponging the diamonds with a glaze mixture.

Photo 4 - Masking off alternate diamonds.

Photo 5 - Sponging the diamonds.

Photo 6 - Mixing paint and glaze to make the lighter-colored glaze mixture.

Photo 7 - Rolling on the lighter-colored glaze on the alternate diamonds.

Finish

Apply two to three coats waterbase polyurethane to inside and outside of bookcase. Let dry between coats. ❑

GRAPES & VINES PIE SAFE

DECORATIVE PAINTING

This grapes and leaves design is perfect for cabinets and looks especially nice when it trails over the door. Chris lined the shelves with a coordinating plaid wallpaper.

If you look closely at this pie safe, you might notice that the door is made from an old window Chris had for sale at her shop, *The Craft Cottage*, in Dallas, Georgia. As you might guess, Chris recycles everything!

By Chris Stokes

SUPPLIES

Project Surface:
Wooden pie safe or other cabinet

Latex paint:
Satin finish for base painting piece
    Warm Yellow

Acrylic craft paints:
For decorative painting design
    Asphaltum
    Black Cherry
    Burnt Sienna
    Burnt Umber
    French Vanilla
    Licorice
    Prussian Blue
    Sap Green
    Turner's Yellow

Paints, Mediums & Finishes:
Oil wood stain, Golden Oak
Waterbase varnish

Brushes:
Flat shade - 3/4"
Stencil brushes *or* round sponge-on-a-stick applicators - 3/4", 1"
Liner
Old toothbrush (for spattering)

Other Supplies:
Sandpaper
Tack cloth
Tracing paper and pencil
Transfer paper and stylus

INSTRUCTIONS

Prepare, Stain & Base Paint
1. Sand cabinet. Wipe away dust with a tack cloth.
2. Stain entire cabinet, inside and out, with Golden Oak stain. Let dry.
3. Thin the latex paint slightly. Paint over stained front, door, and sides with Warm Yellow. The top will remain unpainted and be the stain color. Let dry.

Paint the Design
See the painted example on page 42.
Background:
1. Load a 1" stencil brush with Asphaltum, Sap Green, and Black Cherry by pouncing into each color on different areas of the brush. Pounce this brush onto the surface of your palette to blend the colors and remove some of the excess paint. *Note, pounced paint area will be used later for background leaves.* Blend and rub the colors onto the surface in the area where the design will be painted. (**photo 1**) Let dry.

Continued on page 40

continued from page 38

2. Trace and transfer the design to the surface.

Background Leaves:

1. Find the area on your palette where you pounced the stencil brush to blend the background colors. Add a little water to this puddle to make an inky paint mixture. Using a 3/4" flat shader, load into this color to paint a few inky dark value background ivy leaves. Occasionally load brush into some straight color when reloading (Asphaltum, Sap Green, Black Cherry). (**photo 2**)

2. Paint a few darker leaves by loading the dirty brush into inky Burnt Umber + Burnt Sienna; add Licorice to darken some.

3. Paint a few middle value leaves with Sap Green/Burnt Sienna. Pick up Turner's Yellow on the side of brush to paint some. Pick up Black Cherry on the side of the brush to paint others. (**photo 3**)

Grapes:

1. Multi-load a 3/4" stencil brush by dipping each side into a different color. Use Prussian Blue, Turner's Yellow, and Black Cherry. (**photo 4**)

2. Pounce brush on a palette to blend. (**photo 5**)

3. Paint the grapes, using a twisting motion to make each grape. Add these dark value grapes randomly to the area where the grape bunch will be.

4. Continue adding grapes of other colors using this same technique. Use the following colors:
Medium value grapes - Black Cherry/Turner's Yellow; pick up French Vanilla for some. (**photo 7**)
Light value grapes - Leave the medium grape colors in your brush and pick up more Turner's Yellow/Sap Green; pick up French Vanilla to highlight. (**photo 8**)

Photo 1 - Rubbing in the background.

Photo 2 - Painting the dark value background leaves.

Photo 3 - Painting the middle value background leaves.

Photo 4 - Multi-loading the stencil brush.

Photo 5 - Blending the colors on the stencil brush.

Photo 6 - Painting the dark grapes.

Photo 7 - Painting the medium grapes.

5. Use a 3/4" flat brush to dry brush highlights with French Vanilla. **(photo 9)**
6. Add touches of French Vanilla for reflected light.

Foreground Leaves:
1. Double load a 3/4" flat shader with Sap Green/Asphaltum; tip with French Vanilla. Paint leaves.
2. Add Turner's Yellow and French Vanilla to highlight.
3. Add details to all leaves using a liner brush with inky French Vanilla + a touch of Sap Green. **(photo 10)**

Twigs & Curlicues:
Paint with inky Burnt Umber, using a liner brush. Let dry.

Finish
1. Spatter with inky Burnt Umber. Let dry.
2. Brush with waterbase varnish. Let dry.
3. Rub some areas with Golden Oak stain for an aged effect. Let dry. ❏

Photo 8 - Painting the light grapes.

Photo 9 - Dry brushing highlights on grapes.

Photo 10 - Adding details to foreground leaves.

Painted Example - Grapes & Leaves

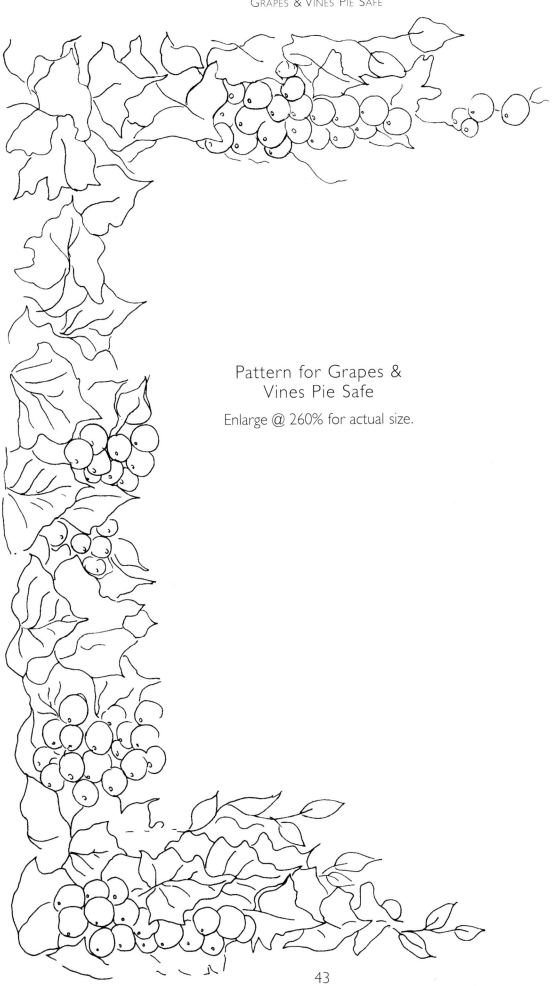

Pattern for Grapes &
Vines Pie Safe

Enlarge @ 260% for actual size.

LEAVES IN A CIRCLE TABLE

STAINING & STAMPING

I found this round table by the side of the road. It had beautiful turned legs but had a scarred, worn top. It was sturdy oak but not very pretty. The legs were given a nice coat of black paint for a contemporary look and the top was stained a dark brown then stamped with a black leaf border.

By Kathi Malarchuk Bailey

SUPPLIES

Project Surface:

Round table with wooden top

Paint, Stains & Finishes:

Latex gloss paint, Black for legs

Wood stain (oil-base or waterbase)

Black

Dark Brown

Polyurethane, satin sheen (Choose oil-base or waterbase, depending on the type of stain.) *Option:* Use gloss sheen for a more durable finish.

Brushes & Tools:

Foam Stamp with leaf motif

Foam brush

Foam roller

Ruler *or* tape measure

Optional: Electric sander

Other Supplies:

Sandpaper, 80 and 220 grits

Tack cloth

Disposable plates

Rags

Marking chalk

Brown paper

INSTRUCTIONS

Prepare

1. Sand top to remove finish and old stain down to bare wood. Use 220 grit sandpaper to sand to smooth.
2. Remove dust with a tack cloth.

Stain

1. Apply Dark Brown stain with a foam brush, working in the direction of the wood grain. (**photo 1**) Wipe off the excess with stain-dampened rags. Let dry two hours.
2. Lightly mark the border placement 3" from the edge all around the table.
3. Apply Black stain to stamp, using a foam roller. (**photo 2**)
4. Press stamp on brown paper first to determine amount of stain needed.
5. Re-load stamp and stamp motifs (**photo 3**) around the table to form a border, using the marks as guides for placement. Alternate the direction of the leaves to create interest. Let dry overnight.

Finish

Seal top with two to three coats of satin varnish. Let dry thoroughly and sand with 220 grit paper between coats.

Option: If a more durable finish is desired, use gloss varnish, following the same instructions. ❏

How-to photos follow on page 46.

continued from page 44

Photo 1 - Applying stain with a foam brush.

Photo 2 - Loading stamp with Black stain, using a foam roller.

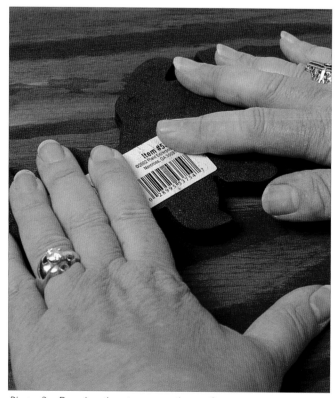

Photo 3 - Pressing the stamp on the surface.

Photo 4 - A stamped motif.

Before

48

Orange Checked Chest

Painting & Stenciling

Kathi added turned wooden legs that she bought at a building supply store to a boxy wooden hinged-top trunk. The length of the legs depends on how tall you want the finished piece to be. Stenciled checks and leaves add design interest to the boxy trunk.

By Kathi Malarchuk Bailey

SUPPLIES

Project Surface:
Wooden trunk with hinged top
4 wooden table legs

Latex paint:
Satin finish for base painting
Off White

Acrylic craft paint:
For stenciling design
Dark Gray
Light Gray
Medium Orange
Red Orange
Yellow Orange

Paints & Finishes:
Primer
Waterbase varnish

Brushes & Tools:
Stencil blank material
Foam brushes
Foam roller
Ruler or tape measure
Craft knife
Stencil brush
Liner brush
Drill
Screwdriver
Optional: Electric sander

Supplies - Stencil blank, pattern, paint, marker for tracing pattern, stencil brush, craft knife, ruler

Other Supplies:
Metal top plates with screws for attaching legs to bottom of chest — must match legs you purchase
Construction adhesive
Sandpaper, 80 and 220 grits
Tack cloth
Disposable plates
Masking tape
Pencil
Black marker

INSTRUCTIONS

Prepare & Prime
1. Sand trunk to remove finish. Use 220 grit sandpaper to smooth.
2. Wipe away dust with a tack cloth.
3. Apply two coats of primer to legs and trunk. Let dry between coats.
4. Attach legs to bottom of trunk with screws. Add construction adhesive for additional support. Let dry.

Base Paint
1. Paint trunk and legs with two coats Off White latex. Let dry thoroughly before continuing.

Continued on next page

continued from page 49

2. Mask off 1-1/2" at top and at bottom of base. Paint with dark gray paint. Let dry. Leave tape on.

3. Mask off 1/4" vertical stripes 1" apart on the two gray bands. Paint with Light Gray. Let dry and remove tape.

4. Measure a band 3" wide around trunk base. Mask off inside that band and inside the gray bands on the top and bottom.

5. Paint the space above and below the Off White band with Yellow Orange. Let dry and remove tape.

Stencil the Checkerboard

1. Trace the checkerboard pattern on stencil blank material. *Tip:* Use a ruler as a guide to make straight lines. (**photo 1**)

2. Cut out, using a craft knife and ruler. (**photo 2**)

3. Position the stencil on the Off White band.

4. Stencil the top and bottom rows of checks around the trunk with Medium Orange, using the stencil brush. (**photo 3**)

5. Re-position the stencil (**photo 4**) to complete the middle row of checks and again, stencil with Medium Orange. Let dry.

Stencil the Leaves

1. Trace the leaf patterns on stencil blank material. Cut out with a craft knife.

2. Stencil large leaves around the checked band, using a stencil brush and Red Orange paint.

3. Stencil the smaller leaves around the top of the trunk, using the stencil brush with Red Orange paint. Use the photo as a guide for placement.

4. Load a liner brush with Red Orange that has been thinned with water. Add stems to leaves and curling tendrils and vines.

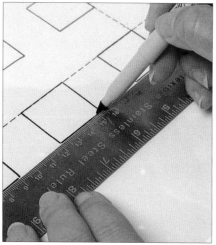
Photo 1 - Tracing the stencil pattern on stencil blank material.

Photo 2 - Cutting the stencil.

Photo 3 - Stenciling the top and bottom rows.

Photo 4 - Re-positioning the stencil before stenciling the middle row.

5. Dip the handle end of the brush in Red Orange and add dots around the top edge. Scatter some dots on the checked band. Let dry.

Finish

1. Trim legs with bands of Yellow Orange, Light Gray, and Red Orange, using the photo as a guide for color placement. Let dry.
2. Apply two to three coats waterbase varnish. Let dry and sand between coats. ❏

Patterns for Stencils
(actual size)

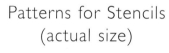

51

ELEGANT CONSOLE TABLE

CRACKLING, STENCILING

Kathi took a castoff wooden wall cabinet with sliding doors and turned it into an elegant-looking console table. The top provides a surface to hold mail and keys, and the cabinet could hold gloves, hats, or handbags in a hallway.

You could use this idea to transform just about any kind of cabinet – this one has sliding doors, but the techniques could also be used on a cabinet with hinged doors.

By Kathi Malarchuk Bailey

SUPPLIES

Project Surface:

Wooden wall cabinet with sliding doors

4 square (Parsons style) wooden legs

Top plates with screws for attaching legs

Luaun plywood, 2 ft. x 2 ft.

Latex paint:

Satin finish for base painting
  Black
  Creamy beige

Other Paints, Mediums & Finishes:

Antiquing medium - Brown

Crackle medium

Acrylic craft paint - Gold

Waterbase polyurethane varnish, satin sheen

Brushes & Tools:

Pre-cut stencil with damask motif

Foam brushes

2" flat bristle brush

Stencil brush

Drill

Saw

Ruler *or* tape measure

Sponge

Optional: Electric sander

Other Supplies:

2 door pulls

Sandpaper, 80 and 220 grits

Tack cloth

Masking tape

Disposable plates

Marking chalk

Screws

Construction adhesive

Continued on page 54

Before

52

continued from page 52

INSTRUCTIONS

Prepare

1. Remove doors. Using them as guides, measure and cut replacements from plywood. Sand to smooth.
2. Sand cabinet to remove finish. Use 220 grit to smooth. Remove dust with tack cloth.
3. Attach legs to bottom of cabinet with metal plates and screws to make the table. Add construction adhesive for additional support. Let dry.

Paint & Crackle Cabinet Base

Set the doors aside for now.

1. Basecoat entire top and legs with two coats Black. Let dry and sand between coats. Let dry completely.
2. Mask off top. Mask off a 1" on all edges of both ends.
3. Apply one to two coats crackle medium. (**photo 1**) Let dry between coats. *Tip:* For larger cracks, apply heavy coats.
4. When crackle medium is dry, use the large bristle brush to apply Creamy Beige on the entire top and on the unmasked areas of the two ends. Work quickly on one area at a time, taking care to NOT overwork the topcoat. Cracks will form. (**photo 2**) Allow to dry thoroughly.
5. Dampen sponge or sponge brush. Dip in Brown antiquing medium. Working one area at a time, apply antiquing over crackled areas on top and ends. Wipe away excess with a rag. (**photo 3**) Let dry. Remove masking tape carefully.

Paint & Stencil the Doors

1. Paint the newly cut doors with two coats Creamy Beige. Let dry and sand between coats. Let dry.
2. Mask off a border 1" wide around all edges. Paint the area inside the

tape with two coats Black. Let dry. Remove tape.
3. Using a dampened sponge, rub Brown antiquing on the Creamy Beige border.
4. Insert doors in cabinet. Lightly mark with a pencil where the front door overlaps the back door. Remove doors.
5. Determine how to place the stencil inside the black area so the stencil appears as one continuous design when both doors are closed. (You may need to mask off or repeat a section of the stencil to achieve the continuous pattern.)
6. Stencil the design with Gold paint on both doors.

Photo 1 - Applying crackle medium to the painted surface.

Photo 2 - Brushing the Creamy Beige topcoat over the crackle medium.

7. Add dots around edges of doors with Gold paint, using the handle end of the stencil brush. Use the photo as a guide for placement. Let paint dry.

Finish

1. Insert doors in cabinet. Add pulls to doors.
2. Seal with waterbase polyurethane. Allow to dry thoroughly before use.
❑

Photo 3 - Wiping off excess antiquing medium.

RED & GOLD DROP LEAF TABLE

PAINTING, GOLD LEAFING

Bright red paint and gleaming gold leaf turn a drop leaf table into a focal point for any room. This table is so stylish that it would look great in a contemporary décor as well as traditional.

By Kathi Malarchuk Bailey

SUPPLIES

Project Surface:

Triangular drop-leaf table with turned legs

Paints & Finishes:

Latex paint - Red

Gray primer

Clear spray gloss lacquer sealer

Brushes & Tools:

Foam brushes

Foam roller

Small bristle brush (to apply adhesive)

Soft bristle brush (for gold leaf)

Optional: Electric sander

Other Supplies:

Imitation gold leaf sheets

Gold leaf adhesive

Sandpaper, 80 and 220 grits

Tack cloth

Disposable plates

Masking tape

Before

INSTRUCTIONS

Prepare

1. Sand table with 80 grit paper to remove finish. Finish with 220 grit to smooth. Remove dust with tack cloth.
2. Apply two coats of primer to entire table. Let dry overnight.

Paint

Apply two to three coats Red latex paint to entire table. Use a foam roller on the flat surfaces for a smooth finish and foam brushes for the legs and crevices. Allow to dry thoroughly.

Apply Gold Leaf

1. Apply masking tape to the areas next to the edge of table and on each side of area of legs where you will gold leaf.
2. Apply leaf adhesive to table edge and bands on legs according to the manufacturer's instructions, using a small bristle brush. Allow to dry until clear and tacky (about 30-60 minutes).
3. Carefully remove one sheet of gold leaf from package. Lay over one area that was coated with adhesive. Use a soft brush to press down. Tear off edge and repeat on the next section, overlapping the leaf slightly. Continue until all areas coated with adhesive are covered.
4. Use the soft brush to stroke over leafed areas, removing rough edges and stray bits of leaf. Use small scraps of leaf to patch any bare spots.

Finish

Spray two to three coats lacquer over the entire table to seal. Let dry between coats. ❑

Patterns for Geranium Chest

Instructions begin on page 61

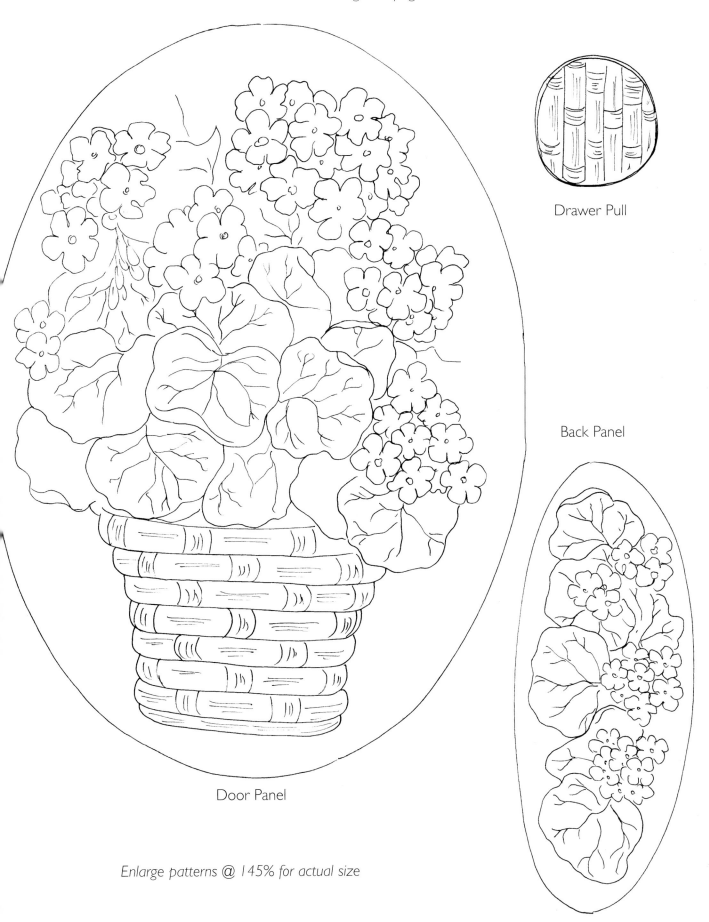

Drawer Pull

Back Panel

Door Panel

Enlarge patterns @ 145% for actual size

GERANIUM CHEST

DECORATIVE PAINTING

This wooden chest was a garage sale find. Chris says her favorite Longaberger basket was her inspiration for the painted raised panel and the door and drawer pulls. On a flat door you could glue on an oval wooden plaque to achieve the same effect.

She liked the original paint color of the piece and chose to sand a few areas for a distressed look before adding the painted designs. If you want to change the base color or your piece hasn't been painted, see the Decorating Techniques sections for instructions on how to create a distressed finish.

By Chris Stokes

Patterns are on page 59

SUPPLIES

Project Surface:
Wooden chest with drawer and door

Acrylic craft paint:
For decorative painting design
- Apple Spice
- Asphaltum
- Burnt Carmine
- Burnt Umber
- Ivory Black
- Red Light
- Sap Green
- Sunflower
- True Burgundy
- Turner's Yellow

Brushes:
Flat shaders - 3/4", #2, #8, #12
Liner
Stencil brush, 3/4"
Foam brushes
Old toothbrush (for spattering)

Other Supplies & Tools:
Waterbase varnish
Tracing paper and pencil
Transfer paper and stylus
Sandpaper

INSTRUCTIONS

Prepare & Base Paint
1. Remove door and drawer pulls. Sand smooth any areas of loose or peeling paint, and sand the edges to create a distressed look. Wipe away dust with a tack cloth.
2. Paint the door panel with overlapping crisscross strokes of Turner's Yellow and Sunflower, using a 3/4" flat brush. Let dry.
3. Shadow floated Asphaltum, working the color toward the oval for an antiqued look.
4. Using an old toothbrush, spatter the panel with inky Burnt Umber.
5. Paint the oval with Ivory Black.
6. Paint the edge of the oval with Apple Spice. Let dry.

Continued on next page

Photo 1 - Painting the vertical slats.

continued from page 61

7. Trace and transfer pattern.

Paint the Design

Basket:

1. Using a #8 flat shader, paint vertical slats with Turner's Yellow + a touch of Asphaltum. (**photo 1**)
2. Paint horizontal slats with Turner's Yellow + a touch of Sunflower. (**photo 2**)
3. Shade slats with floated Asphaltum. (**photo 3**)
4. Outline slats with inky Ivory Black.
5. Highlight with inky Sunflower.
6. Repeat steps 1-5 to paint the basketweave design on the pulls.

Geranium Leaves:

1. Multi-load a #12 flat shader by first dipping a corner into Sap Green first. (**photo 4**) Dip a corner into True Burgundy (**photo 5**). Then dip the same corner into Turner's Yellow (**photo 6**). Blend gently on your palette. (**photo 7**)

Continued on page 64

Photo 2 - Painting the horizontal slats.

Photo 3 - Shading the slats with Asphaltum.

continued from pag 63

2. Using a wiggle motion, pull brush around in a heart shape with a rounded bottom to create a leaf shape (**photo 8**) Let dry.
3. Use the same dirty brush and pick up Sunflower on the corner. Add highlights to edges of leaves with this brush. (**photo 9**)
4. Outline leaves randomly with inky Sunflower, using a liner brush.
5. Paint veins with inky Burnt Umber, using a liner brush. (**photo 10**)

Geranium Flowers:
1. Multi-load the stencil brush with True Burgundy, Burnt Carmine, and Apple Spice. Pounce in flower area. Let dry.
2. Double-load #8 and #4 flats to paint the five-petal flowers with these color combinations:

Photo 4 - Loading the brush with Sap Green.

Photo 5 - Loading the brush with True Burgundy.

Photo 6 - Loading the brush with Turner's Yellow.

Photo 7 - Blending on the palette.

Photo 8 - Wiggling in a leaf.

Photo 9 - Highlighting with Sunflower.

Photo 10 - Painting the veins.

Burnt Carmine and True Burgundy
True Burgundy and Apple Spice
Apple Spice and Turner's Yellow
Pick up Sunflower on foreground flowers.
3. Using a liner brush, dot centers with Burnt Carmine.
4. Highlight centers with Turner's Yellow.
5. Using a liner brush with inky Sunflower, randomly outline some flowers.

Twigs & Stems:
Using a liner brush with inky Sunflower paint, wiggle in twigs and stems.

Finish
1. Apply two coats of waterbase varnish to the cabinet and the pulls. Let dry.
2. Replace pulls. ❏

FALL LEAVES TRAY TABLE

DECORATIVE PAINTING

You can find these wooden tray tables with folding legs at discount stores as well as in antique and gift shops and at flea markets and yard sales.

To create this design, Chris collected fall leaves from her yard, pressed them in a photo album, and referred to them as she painted. Chris says you could also paint parts of the design on cabinet doors, a welcome sign, or a plate (as shown in the photo). Remember that painted plates are for decorative purposes only! After painting, seal the plate with glass sealer.

By Chris Stokes

SUPPLIES

Project Surface:
Wooden tray table

Latex wall paint:
Satin finish for base painting
　Raspberry color

Acrylic craft paint:
For decorative painting design
　Burnt Carmine
　Burnt Umber
　Ivory Black
　Linen
　Olive Green
　Prussian Blue
　Raspberry Wine
　Red Orange
　Sap Green
　Taffy
　Transparent Oxide Red
　Yellow Ochre

Brushes:
Flat shaders - 3/4", #12
Liner
Stencil brushes - small, medium
　(for berries)
Round - #5

Tools & Other Supplies:
Clear spray sealer, satin sheen
Large piece of tissue paper
Foam roller

INSTRUCTIONS

Base Paint & Add Texture

1. Base paint entire tray with Raspberry. Let dry.
2. Paint the oval area in center of tray with a heavy coat of Linen. While paint is still wet, paint on some steaks of Taffy paint in a slip slapping motion and applying the paint fairly thick. (**photo 1**)

Continued on page 68

continued from page 67

3. While paint is still wet, place a piece of tissue paper over the oval area. Using a paint roller, roll the tissue paper into the wet paint (the more wrinkles the better!). (**photo 2**) Carefully pull off the tissue – you'll reveal a textured area. Let dry.

4. Shade the edge of the oval with Olive Green. To do this, use the same dirty brush you used to base paint the oval, loading a corner of it with Olive Green. (**photo 3**)

5. Shade again with a small amount of Raspberry Wine + Yellow Ochre.

Paint the Design

Vines & Twigs:
Using a #5 round, paint vines and branches with inky Burnt Umber + Olive Green.

Sumac Leaves:
These are red-burgundy leaves on the long branches.
Using a #12 flat double loaded with Olive Green/Raspberry Wine, paint the leaves. Pick up Red Orange and Burnt Carmine as you paint.

Virginia Creeper Leaves:
These are the stems with five-leaf clusters.
1. Double load the #12 flat with Red Orange/Transparent Red Oxide and paint some of the leaves.
2. Paint others with Olive Green/Yellow Ochre.
3. Highlight with touches of Taffy.

Rusty Orange Leaves:
1. Multi-load a #12 flat with Transparent Oxide Red/Red Orange/Yellow Light and paint leaves.
2. Highlight with Taffy.

Ivy Leaves:
Load the #12 flat shader with Sap Green + a touch of Burnt Umber and Yellow Light + a touch of Taffy. Paint ivy leaves.

Photo 1 - Painting the oval with Linen and Taffy, slip-slapping the paint on fairly thick.

Photo 2 - Rolling the tissue paper into the wet paint.

Photo 3 - Shading the oval with Olive Green.

Gold Maple Leaves:
Multi-load 3/4" flat brush with Yellow Ochre and Olive Green/Taffy. Pick up a tad of Red Orange. Paint maple leaves.

Pyracantha Berries:
These are the orange ones.
1. Multi-load a small stencil brush with Olive Green + a touch of Red Orange and Taffy. Pounce on your palette to blend the colors. Using a twisting motion, paint the berries.
2. Add touches of Yellow Light and Taffy to highlight.
3. Dot the blossom ends with Ivory Black, using a liner brush.

Blueberries:
1. Load a medium stencil brush with Prussian Blue + a touch of Raspberry Wine and Taffy. Pounce on a palette to blend the colors. Using a twisting motion, paint the berries.
2. Dot the blossom ends with Ivory Black.
3. Add dots of Taffy to highlight.

Veins & Branches:
Don't forget to wiggle that brush!
1. Paint veins in leaves with inky Burnt Umber. Pick up a little Taffy to highlight.
2. Add a few more branches with the same colors.

Finish
1. Add a tiny touch of Burnt Umber to inky Yellow ochre. Spatter the tray, using an old toothbrush. Let dry.
2. Seal with satin spray sealer. Let dry. ❏

Closeup view of tray table design

Section A

Pattern for Fall Leaves
Tray Table

Enlarge @ 135% for actual size.

Section B

Connect Section A to Section B at
dotted lines to complete pattern.

Bee Skep Storage Bench

DECORATIVE PAINTING

This old storage bench was given new life with this primitive-style painting on the front. This piece looks great in a hall, sitting room, or bedroom.

By Kathleen Taylor

Instructions begin on page 74.

BEE SKEP STORAGE BENCH

SUPPLIES

Painting Surface:
Wood blanket bench

Acrylic craft paint:
For decorative painting
 Baby Blue
 Coffee Bean
 English Mustard
 French Blue
 Green Light
 Green Medium
 Grass Green
 Lime Light
 Naphthol Crimson
 Pink
 Poppy Red
 Raw Umber
 Sap Green
 Sunflower
 Sweetheart Pink
 Teddy Bear Tan
 Yellow Ochre

Artist Brushes:
Kathleen keeps a variety of sizes of round and flat artist brushes on hand. Use the size you are most comfortable with for each area of the design.

Other Paints & Finishes:
Indoor/outdoor acrylic enamel for base painting, Mustard
Outdoor sealer, satin sheen

Tools & Other Supplies:
Stencil brush - 1/2"
Pre-cut checkerboard stencils
Stencil tape
Stencil blanks material (for cutting optional stencil)
Utility or craft knife (for cutting optional stencil)
Painter's masking tape
Ruler

INSTRUCTIONS

Prepare
1. Prepare bench by sanding.
2. Base paint with Mustard. Let dry.
3. Paint rims of lid, box bottom rim, and sides of legs with a Baby Blue wash.
4. Draw a line 2" above bottom edge of box. Place tape along the ruled line on box front with the bottom edge of the tape on the line. Fill in area below line and above the bottom rim with French Blue, using the stencil brush.
5. Trace the design and transfer it to the surface above the French Blue band.

Paint the Design
Checkerboard Top:
1. Find and mark center of box lid.
2. Turn the checkerboard stencil diagonally to create a diamond pattern and place the center of the stencil over the center mark. Tape in place.
3. Stencil the pattern with Lime Light, using the stencil brush. Reposition the stencil as needed.

Pattern on Blue Band:
If desired, cut a stencil of this all-over pattern for quicker and more uniform painting.
Paint or stencil the design on the French Blue band with Baby Blue.

Bee Skep:
1. Basecoat with English Mustard.

2. Shade each side and outline the layers with a Coffee Bean wash.
3. Paint the diagonal lines on each layer with Teddy Bear Tan.
4. Paint the entrance with Coffee Bean. Shade with Raw Umber.

Leaves:
1. Basecoat with Green Medium. Let dry.
2. Paint one half of each leaf with Grass Green.
3. Paint leaf stems and veins and outline leaves with Sap Green.

Flowers:
1. Basecoat with Poppy Red.
2. Paint stitch lines outlining flowers with Sweetheart Pink.
3. Paint centers with Pink. Outline centers with Naphthol Crimson.
4. Paint dots on centers with Sunflower.

Trees:
1. Paint trunks with Coffee Bean.
2. Outline trunks with Raw Umber.
3. Basecoat leaves with Sap Green.
4. Highlight leaves with Green Light.

Bumblebees:
1. Paint wings with Wicker White.
2. Paint bodies and antennae with Raw Umber. Let dry.
3. Paint stripes on bodies with Yellow Ochre. Let dry.

Finish
Varnish with Outdoor Sealer. ❏

Pattern for Bee Skep & Bee
(actual size)

Bee Skep
Place at center.

Pattern for Tree
(actual size)

Pattern for Flower
(actual size)

Reverse and repeat on opposite side of tree.

Pattern for Bottom Band
(actual size)

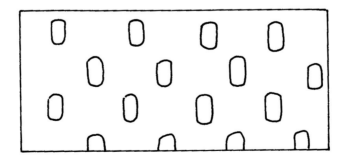

Option: Cut a stencil for quick, easy painting.

ROSE ARMOIRE

DECORATIVE PAINTING

This project was painted on an antique armoire with one door. The door has two recessed panels. The armoire was painted green when Kathleen acquired it so she did only minor sanding to the piece before beginning the painted design.

By Kathleen Taylor

SUPPLIES

Project Surface:

Wooden armoire with paneled door

Acrylic craft paint:

For decorative painting design

Bayberry

Burnt Umber

Butter Pecan

Buttercup

Fuchsia

Green Umber

Lemonade

Lime Yellow

Mystic Green

Purple Passion

Rose Pink

Sterling Blue

Warm White

Yellow Ochre

Artist Brushes:

Kathleen keeps a variety of sizes of round and flat artist brushes on hand. Use the size you are most comfortable with for each area of the design.

Tools & Other Supplies:

Dark green latex paint for base

painting *optional*

Polyurethane varnish, matte sheen

Paint brushes

Sandpaper

Tack cloth

Rags

INSTRUCTIONS

Prepare & Base Paint

1. *Option:* Paint the armoire with dark green paint. Let dry.
2. Lightly sand the painted surface for a worn look. Wipe away dust with a tack cloth.
3. Make a color wash with Mystic Green and brush over the painted surface, wiping off any excess.
4. Paint the recessed panels with Purple Passion.
5. Paint the border of each panel with Yellow Ochre.
6. Trace and transfer the diamond border to the front of the cabinet around the door.
7. Paint the diamond border with Sterling Blue.
8. Trace the rose pattern and transfer to the center of each panel.

Paint the Design

Roses:

1. Basecoat the roses with Fuchsia.

2. Wash with rose pink.
3. Paint the flower centers with Butter Pecan.
4. Fill in the accent outlines of the petals with equal amounts of Fuchsia + Warm White.
5. Accent the flower centers with Warm White.
6. Paint the dots with a mix of Buttercup + Lemonade.

Stems:

1. Paint the rose stems with Lime Yellow.
2. Trace an accent line on one side of each stem with Warm White.

Leaves & Stems:

1. Basecoat each leaf with Bayberry.
2. Paint veins with Lime Yellow.
3. Paint thorns on the stems with Butter Pecan.
4. Accent each thorn with a wash of Green Umber.

Finish

1. Lightly sand edges of door, cabinet, and edges of recessed panels.
2. Make a color wash of two parts Burnt Umber and one part water. Brush over entire cabinet, making sure the sanded areas get covered well. Wipe off excess. Let dry.
3. Seal cabinet with matte polyurethane. Let dry. ❏

Section 1

Patterns for Rose Armoire
Enlarge @ 135% for actual size.

Section 2

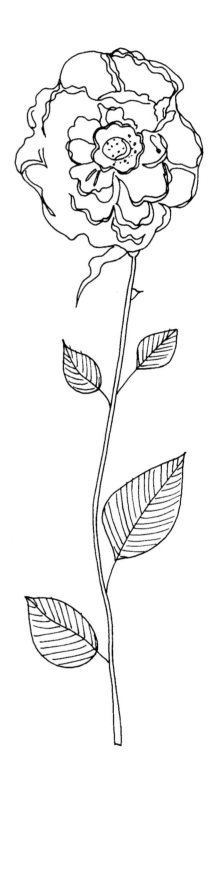

Section 3

Border (actual size)

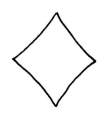

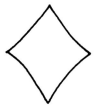

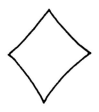

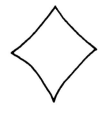

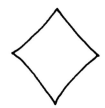

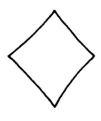

BABY MEMORIES PHOTO SCREEN

PAINTING, DECOUPAGE

Photocopies or digital prints of family photos are decoupaged to a folding screen and surrounded by lacy-looking clip art frames, which are also decoupaged. What a great idea for a child's room or a wonderful gift for Grandma!

By Kathi Malarchuk Bailey

SUPPLIES

Project Surface:

Three-panel wooden folding screen

Latex paints:

Satin finish for base painting

Light Yellow

Muted Green

White

Brushes & Tools:

Clear spray sealer, matte sheen

Foam brushes

Foam roller

Craft knife

Ruler

Pencil

Other Supplies:

Decoupage medium

Baby photos — you can use color photos copies and keep the originals

Paper frames, motifs, and borders (clip art provided)

Sandpaper, 80 and 220 grits

Tack cloth

Masking tape

Disposable plates

INSTRUCTIONS

Prepare

1. Remove hinges and set aside.
2. Sand screen to remove old finish. Remove dust with tack cloth.
3. Make color photocopies or digital prints on copy paper of baby pictures, enlarging or reducing them to fit the screen panels.
4. Photocopy the frames, motifs, and borders, enlarging as needed to fit screen panels.
5. Trim copies of photos to fit inside paper frames.
6. Spray all color pictures with matte spray to seal.

Paint

1. Paint the center area of each panel with two coats White. Let dry.
2. Mask edges of white areas and paint trim with two coats Muted Green. Let dry and remove tape.
3. Measure width of panel and divide into vertical stripes of equal width. (Our panel is 10" wide and was divided into five 2" stripes.)
4. Mask every other stripe. Paint alternating stripes with Light Yellow. Let dry and remove tape.
5. Use 80 grit sandpaper to sand painted stripes for a distressed look. Wipe away dust.

Decoupage

1. Cut out borders and lay out on four edges of each panel.
2. Apply decoupage medium to back of each border and adhere to surface, pressing carefully to remove air bubbles. Continue trim around entire panel. Repeat for each panel.
3. Match pictures to frames. Cut out frame centers, using a craft knife and ruler.
4. Cut out motifs to make the "ribbons" that connect the framed photos.
5. Mark the center of the width of each panel with pencil to use as a guide for picture and ribbon placement.
6. Lay out framed pictures and ribbons for each panel, marking the placement with a pencil.
7. Apply decoupage medium to the back of each picture and adhere to the panel, using placement marks as guides. Continue until all pictures are adhered. Add frames over pictures and ribbon motifs to link the frames.

Finish

1. Erase all visible pencil lines.
2. Brush each panel with two coats decoupage medium, using a foam brush.
3. Re-attach hinges to panels and panels to each other. ❑

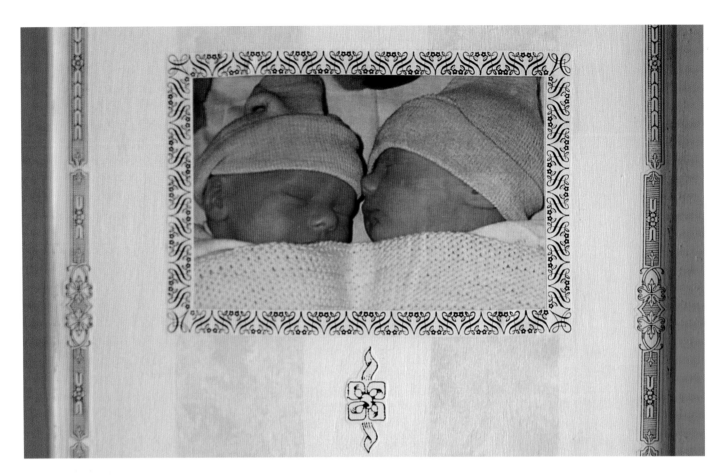

Clip Art for decoupage

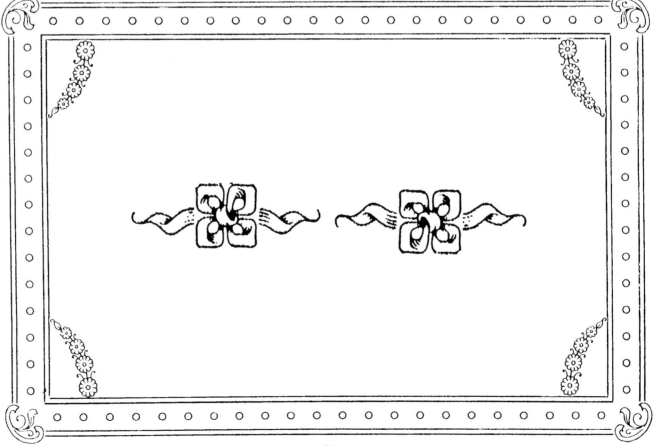

Baby Memories Photo Screen

RETRO KITCHEN CHAIRS

DECORATIVE PAINTING, STENCILING

When Kathi decided to give her kitchen a retro 50s look, she could find the paint colors she wanted but not the fabric. Her solution was to create her own fabric by stenciling and painting on canvas cloth. She created two designs—a stripe and a fruit and flowers print—that she used to cover the seats of her ladderback kitchen chairs, then painted more fabric and used it to make matching cafe curtains for the kitchen windows.

By Kathi Malarchuk Bailey

SUPPLIES

Project Surface:

Wooden ladderback kitchen chairs

Latex paint:

Satin finish for base painting

    Aqua

    White

Acrylic craft paint or stencil paint:

For decorative painting and stenciling

    Black

    Green

    Russet

    Yellow

    Brown

Mediums & Finishes:

White primer

Textile medium

Spray matte sealer

Brushes & Tools:

Foam brushes

Staple gun

Scissors

Craft knife

Artist's round brush

Other Supplies:

Pre-cut stencil with citrus motifs

2" thick foam (to cover chair seats)

2 yds. white canvas fabric to cover foam and seats

Sandpaper, 80 and 220 grits

Tack cloth

Masking tape

Disposable plates

Transfer paper and stylus

Tracing paper and pencil

INSTRUCTIONS

Prepare & Prime

1. Sand chairs to remove finish. Use 220 grit to sand smooth. Remove dust with tack cloth.
2. Apply two coats white primer. Let dry between coats. Let second coat dry thoroughly.

Paint the Chairs

1. Paint chairs with two coats of Aqua. Let dry thoroughly.
2. Mask off alternating rungs on backs of chairs and paint with White. Let dry and remove tape.
3. Measure and mark centers of white rungs. Mask off a 1" stripe down the center of each. Paint yellow and remove tape. Outline with black paint.
4. Trace and transfer pattern to back and front of chair backs, mirroring the pattern for either side of center.
5. Paint large swirls with Aqua, using a round brush.
6. Use the handle end of the brush to make scattered Black dots.

Continued on page 90

continued from page 88

Paint & Cover the Chair Seats

1. Cut foam to fit over chair seat. Cut fabric to fit over foam, allowing at least 2-3" of extra of fabric on each side to be anchored underneath the chair.
2. Mix paints with textile medium according to the textile medium manufacturer's instructions.
3. For fruit and flowers design, stencil fabric using the citrus stencil with these colors:
   Leaves - Green
   Lemons- Yellow, Green, Russet
   Twigs- Brown
   Flowers - Aqua, Yellow

4. For a striped seat, measure, mark, and mask off vertical stripes on the fabric and paint. On this seat, the Yellow stripes are 1-1/2" wide, the Aqua stripes are 1/4" wide, and the White stripes are 1" wide. Let dry and remove masking tape.

Finish

1. Spray chairs with matte sealer. Let dry.
2. Place foam on chair seat. Place painted fabric over foam. Staple fabric to underside of chair seat, using a staple gun. Pull the fabric tightly a you work, starting at the center front, alternating the stapling front to back, then side to side for an even fit. ❏

Pattern for Chair Back
(actual size)

TEEN PRINCESS NIGHTSTAND

DECORATIVE PAINTING

This French provincial-style two-drawer nightstand was part of a furniture grouping that Karen's daughter had as a child. She wanted to update the look with bright colors now that her daughter is a teenager. Wow has this piece changed! Retro-look glass drawer pulls let the paint colors and designs show through. Painting can allow you to change any piece of furniture into the style you want.

By Karen Embry

SUPPLIES

Project Surface:

Two-drawer wooden nightstand

Acrylic craft paints:

For decorative painting the design

Bright Pink

Engine Red

Fresh Foliage

Green Medium

Inca Gold (Metallic)

Medium Yellow

Patina

Pink

Pumpkin

Pure Black

Pure Orange

Purple Lilac

Wicker White

Yellow Citron

Paint Brushes:

Round - #4, #6

Liner - #2, #4

Before

Tools & Other Supplies:

White primer

White latex wall paint in a satin finish for base painting piece

Waterbase varnish

Opaque black paint marker

Sandpaper

Tack cloth

Sponge roller

Transfer paper

Fine red glitter

Hologram glitter

2 glass drawer pulls

Thick and tacky glue

INSTRUCTIONS

Prepare & Base Paint

1. Remove drawer pulls. Clean away all grease and dirt residue; wipe dry with a cotton rag or cloth.
2. Sand with sand paper to create a "tooth" so paint will adhere. Wipe with a tack cloth.
3. Apply a good coat of primer to prevent old paint, stains, and imperfections from seeping through to your new designs.
4. Base paint with White latex paint. Let dry.
5. Paint the top (but not the rim) with Yellow Citron acrylic craft paint.
6. Basecoat the panels on the sides with Purple Lilac acrylic craft paint. Let dry.
7. Trace and transfer the designs to the top and sides.

Paint the Top

1. Paint the crown with Inca Gold.
2. Paint the diamonds on the points of the crown with Purple Lilac, Bright Pink, and Medium Yellow.
3. Paint the band on the diamond ring with Inca Gold. Paint the diamond on the ring with Wicker White.

Continued on page 94

continued from page 92

4. Paint the larger heart with Bright Pink. Paint the smaller heart with Pink.
5. Paint the flower closest to the hearts with Medium Yellow. Paint the center of this flower with Pure Orange.
6. Paint the flower closest to the crown with Purple Lilac. Paint the center of this flower with Medium Yellow.
7. Paint the remaining five-petal flower with Patina. Paint the center with Purple Lilac.
8. Paint the tulip with Engine Red.
9. Paint the roses with Bright Pink. Paint the centers with Pink.
10. Paint the leaves with Green Medium.

Paint the Right Side

1. Paint the moon with Medium Yel-low. Paint the small star with Patina.
2. Paint the large star with Pure Orange. Paint the trim on the ends of the star with Medium Yellow.
3. Paint the shoe with Engine Red. Paint the inside of the shoe with Pink.
4. Paint the cake with Wicker White.
5. Paint the icing and roses with Pink. Paint a Bright Pink swirl in the centers of the roses.
6. Paint the leaves with Fresh Foliage.
7. Paint the candles with Bright Pink. Paint the candle flames with Medium Yellow.
8. Paint the heart with Engine Red. Paint dots in the center of the heart with Wicker White.

Paint the Left side

1. Paint the center of the sun with Pumpkin. Paint the rays of the sun with Medium Yellow.
2. Paint the bird with Patina. Paint the bird's beak with Medium Yellow.
3. Paint the bee's body with Medium Yellow. Paint the stripes on the bee's body with Pure Black.
4. Paint the bee's wings with Wicker White. Paint the bee's eye with Pure Black.
5. Paint the butterfly's wings with Pure Orange. Paint the butterfly's body with Medium Yellow. Paint the designs on the wings with Medium Yellow, Purple Lilac, and Fresh Foliage.
6. Paint the flower with Bright Pink. Paint the center of the flower with Pink. Paint the leaves with Fresh Foliage.

Paint the Drawer Fronts
Top Drawer:
1. Paint the outer trim with Yellow Citron.
2. Paint the next section with Pink.

Continued on page 96

Enlarge @225% for actual size.

Love

Princess today... Queen tomorrow

Believe in miracles.

laugh

Rings-Things.

Dream

Flowers

continued from page 94

3. Paint the panel with Coastal Blue.

4. Paint the star with Medium Yellow.

5. Paint the flower with Pure Orange. Paint the flower center with Engine Red.

Bottom Drawer:

1. Paint the outer trim with Medium Yellow.

2. Paint the next section with Purple Lilac.

3. Paint the panel with Pure Orange.

4. Paint the lips with Engine Red.

5. Paint the flower petals with Bright Pink. Paint the flower center with Coastal Blue. Paint the leaf with Fresh Foliage.

Paint the Legs & Trim

1. Paint the curved areas of the front legs with Medium Yellow. Add dots with Engine Red.

2. Paint the curved corner panels with Bright Pink. Add dots with Wicker White.

3. Paint the checks on the edges of the top and the drawers with Pure Black. Let dry.

Finish

1. Brush a thin coat of glue on the red area of the red shoe on the right side and on the stone of the diamond ring on the top. While glue is wet, sprinkle red glitter on the shoe and hologram glitter on the diamond. Let dry and brush off the excess.

2. Brush a coat of varnish on the glittered areas only. Let dry completely.

3. Brush two coats of varnish on the entire nightstand. Let dry completely.

4. Outline all designs with the black paint marker. Let dry.

5. Attach new drawer pulls to the drawer fronts. ❑

Pattern for Right Side

Enlarge @165% for actual size.

Use photo as a guide
for placement.

Patterns for Drawers
Enlarge @ 180% for actual size.

Patterns for Drawers   *Enlarge @ 165% for actual size.*

GECKO TABLE

DECORATIVE PAINTING

A simple, stylized design and a sophisticated color scheme turn an ordinary-looking occasional table into a great-looking accent piece.

By Karen Embry

SUPPLIES

Acrylic craft paint:

For decorative painting design

Dapple Gray

Italian Sage

Tapioca

Finishes:

Waterbase varnish

Waterbase white primer

Paint Brushes:

Liners - #2, #4

Square Wash - size 1"

Round - #2, #6

Tools & Other Supplies:

Sandpaper

Tack cloth

Tracing paper

Transfer paper

Brass drawer pull

Cotton rags

Masking tape

Before

INSTRUCTIONS

Prepare & Base Paint

1. Remove old drawer pull.
2. Remove all grease and dirt residue. Wipe surface with a cotton rag or cloth.
3. Sand with sandpaper to create a "tooth" so paint will adhere to your surface. Wipe with a tack cloth.
4. Apply a good coat of primer to prevent old stains and imperfections from showing through your new design.

5. Base paint the top of the table, the table apron, and the bottom shelf with Tapioca.
6. Base paint table legs and drawer front with Italian Sage. Let dry.
7. Trace and transfer the design.

Paint the Design

1. Mask off and paint the rectangle on the tabletop and the trim at the edge of the top with Italian Sage. Let dry and remove tape.
2. Paint the gecko lizards, swirls, and zig-zag designs with Italian Sage. Let dry.
3. Paint the thin lines on the edges of the lizards, swirls, and zig-zag designs with Dapple Gray. Let dry.

Finish

1. Trim table legs with Tapioca, using photo as a guide for color placement. Let dry.
2. Brush on two coats of varnish. Let dry between coats.
3. When second coat of varnish is thoroughly dry, attach new drawer pull. ❑

Closeup view - top of table.

Pattern for Gecko Table

Enlarge @180% for actual size.

VICTORIAN-INSPIRED UPHOLSTERED CHAIR

DECORATIVE PAINTING ON FABRIC

The fabric on this upholstered chair was in good shape but very stained so Chris painted stripes and, on the back, a pretty flowered doily. Now it has a whole new look! Before you start, test the effect of the paint on your chair. (Of course, you can always re-upholster – so what have you got to lose?)

By Chris Stokes

SUPPLIES

Project Surface:

Old upholstered chair with wooden arms and legs

Acrylic craft paint:

For decorative painting design

Ballet Pink	Burnt Umber
English Mustard	Poetry Green
Porcelain Blue	Potpourri Rose
Teal Green	Warm White

Brushes:

Flat shaders - #8, #12

Liner - 10/0

Stencil brush - 1"

Other Supplies:

Textile medium

Optional: Waterbase varnish

Masking tape

Sandpaper

Tack cloth

INSTRUCTIONS

Prepare

1. Vacuum fabric well.
2. Sand any loose paint from the wooden arms, apron, and legs for a distressed look, being careful not to abrade the fabric. Wipe away sanding dust.
3. Using masking tape, tape off 1-1/4" stripes. Tape off doily area above stripes. (No stripes are painted in this area.)

Paint the Design

Stripes & Doily Area:

1. Using a 1" stencil brush dipped in textile medium, load brush with Ballet Pink and Potpourri Rose and fill in striped areas (this will look streaky). Let dry a few minutes.
2. Pick up Ballet Pink and pull highlights on top of the stripes (this will look like shiny satin). Let dry.
3. Tape over stripes below doily line.
4. Using the 1" stencil brush loaded with textile medium and Warm White, paint doily area. Let dry.
5. Load a #8 flat shader with Ballet Pink + a touch of Potpourri Rose. Paint the ribbon trim around edge of doily, leaving 1/4" between 1-1/4" sections of ribbon. Let dry.
6. Outline doily with Burnt Umber.
7. Use a liner brush to pull Ballet Pink highlights on the sections of ribbon trim.

Background Leaves:

1. Double load the #8 flat shader with inky Poetry Green. Pull a few small leaves.
2. Pick up inky Teal Green and inky Warm White and pull a few more leaves for depth.

Roses:

1. Stroke rose petals, using a double loaded #12 flat shader with Potpourri Rose and Ballet Pink.

Pick up Warm White to pull highlights.
2. Float a tad of Teal Green to shade.
3. Add a few dots of English Mustard and Warm White in center of each rose.

Blue Flowers:

1. Paint two layers of petals: Double load Porcelain Blue and Warm White and wiggle in five bottom petals. Paint in five smaller top petals. Flip a few over with Warm White.
2. Pounce center with English Mustard + a tad of Teal Green. Highlight with Warm White.
3. Paint tiny blue flowers the same way, using a #8 flat shader.

Gold Flowers:

Paint five-petal flowers with double loaded English Mustard and Warm White, using a #8 flat shader.

Foreground Leaves:

1. Double load a #12 flat shader with Teal Green and Poetry Green. Wiggle in leaves.
2. Pick up Warm White to highlight.

Curlicues:

Paint with inky English Mustard, using a liner brush.

Finish

Option: Apply varnish to the wooden parts of the chair. Let dry. ❑

Pattern for Rose Garland Lamp

(actual size) *Instructions begin on page 108.*

Connect Sections A
and Sections B at
dotted lines to
complete patterns.

Section A

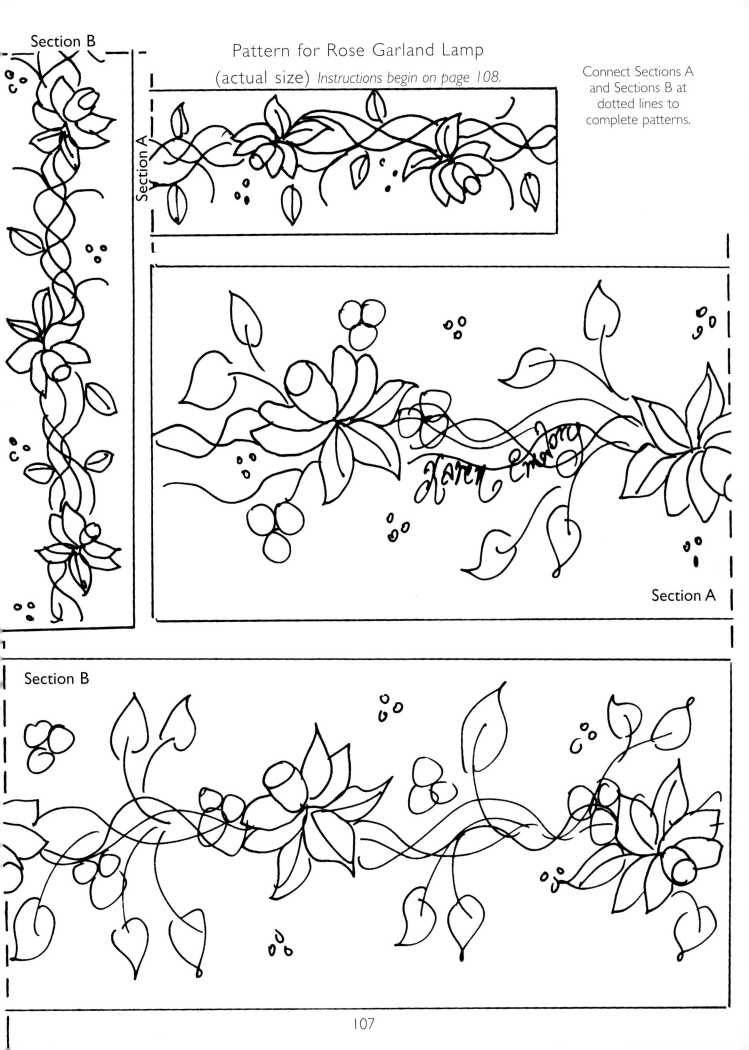

Section A

Section B

ROSE GARLAND LAMP

DECORATIVE PAINTING

This lamp is made of brass (including the shade) that was tarnished and not very nice looking. A painted design greatly changes its look, giving it a decidedly romantic appeal.

By Karen Embry

Patterns are on page 107

SUPPLIES

Project Surface:

Brass table lamp

Acrylic craft paint:

For decorative painting design

Almond Parfait

Basil Green

Barnyard Red

Butter Pecan

Ice Green Light

Linen

Pure Gold (Metallic)

Warm White

Brushes:

Brights - #2, #6, #10

Wash - 1"

Liner - #2, #4

Other Supplies:

Waterbase white primer

Waterbase varnish

Tracing paper and pencil

Transfer paper and stylus

Fine sandpaper (400 grit)

Tack cloth

Sea sponge

Ornamental pearl trim

Thick and tacky glue

Household cleaner

Before

INSTRUCTIONS

Prepare & Prime

1. Use a household cleaner to remove grease and dirt from the base and shade.
2. Sand lightly with 400 grit sandpaper. Wipe with a tack cloth.
3. Apply a good coat of primer. Let dry.

Base Paint

1. Using the sea sponge, sponge the shade with Basil Green + Warm White.
2. Paint the trim at the base of the shade with Pure Gold.
3. Beginning with the top section of the lamp base, paint each section, working from top to bottom, with the colors listed. Adjust the sequence of colors as needed to fit your lamp base.
   Top section - Basil Green
   Next band - Pure Gold
   Next band - Basil Green
   Next band - Pure Gold
   Next small band - Ice Green Light
   Next band (the one with small flowers painted on it) - Basil Green
   Next band - Pure Gold
   Next band: Ice Green Light
   Next band (the one with large flowers painted on it) - Basil Green
   Next band - Pure Gold
   Last band (at the bottom of the base) - Basil Green
4. Trace and transfer the design.

Paint the Design

1. Paint the vine behind the large roses with Butter Pecan + Linen.
2. Paint the large roses with Butter Pecan and Warm White.
3. Paint the small flowers with Barnyard Red and Almond Parfait.
4. Paint the leaves with Butter Pecan and Linen.
5. Paint the dots with Almond Parfait. Let dry.

Finish

1. Brush on one coat of varnish. Let dry.
2. Glue on pearl trim to lamp shade and lamp base. ❑

BUNNY IN THE GARDEN TABLE

DECORATIVE PAINTING

This cute bunny is easy to paint and would add a bit of whimsy and humor to any room. I love to add an element of surprise to each room by pairing informal and formal pieces together.

By Holly Buttimer

SUPPLIES

Project Surface:
Round pedestal table

Acrylic craft paint:
For decorative painting the design (see color chart for list of colors)

Tools & Other Supplies:
Waterbase varnish
Paint comb
Tracing paper and pencil
Transfer paper and stylus
Paint brushes
Sandpaper
Tack cloth

INSTRUCTIONS

Prepare, Base Paint & Comb
1. Sand surface until smooth. Wipe away dust with a tack cloth.
2. Base paint top of table with Light Blue.
3. Paint edges of table and base with Lime Green. Let dry.
4. Brush Olive Green over Lime Green and, while paint is wet, comb with a paint comb.

Continued on page 113

COLOR CHART

Light Blue	Black	Yellow	Raspberry Red
Light Pink	Orange	Poppy Red	Buckskin Brown
Pure Gold (Metallic)	Lime Green	Fresh Foliage	Peridot (Metallic)
Olive Green	Sea Green	Orchid	White
Gray			

BUNNY IN THE GARDEN TABLE

Pattern for Table Top

Enlarge @135% for actual size.

Connect Section A to Section B at dotted
lines to complete pattern.

Section A

Section B

continued from page 110

5. Accent the turned pedestal and base with stripes of various colors and Black and White checks, using the photo as a guide.
6. Trace the pattern and transfer the design to the tabletop.

Paint the Design

Rabbit:
1. Paint the body with Black and White. Shade with Gray.
2. Paint inside ears with Light Pink. Shade with Buckskin Brown and Orchid.
3. Paint eyes with Buckskin Brown. Paint pupils with Black. Highlight with White.

Butterfly:
1. Paint butterfly's wings with Orange. Add highlights with Yellow and White.
2. Shade wings with Pure Gold and Buckskin Brown.
3. Outline, detail, and paint antennae with Black.
4. Paint body with Black. Add White highlights.

Ladybug:
1. Paint ladybug with Black and Poppy Red.
2. Add White highlights.

Bee:
1. Paint bee's body with Yellow and Black.
2. Paint wings with White.
3. Outline, paint head, antennae and legs, and add details with Black.

Roses:
1. Paint roses with Light Pink and Raspberry Red.
2. Highlight with White. Trim with Black.

Leaves & Grass:
Paint with various shades of green—Lime Green, Fresh Foliage, Olive Green, and Peridot.

Daisies:
1. Paint petals with White.
2. Paint centers with Yellow and Orange. Let dry.

Finish
Seal with waterbase varnish. Let dry. ❑

BIRD'S NEST CHILD'S CHAIR

DECORATIVE PAINTING

Chris thought this child's school desk chair was just too cute to pass up when she spotted it at a flea market. And now that she has granddaughters, she is always looking for furniture she can paint for them when they come to visit. It was painted a cream color when she found it, and she chose to keep the worn-looking paint as a background. What a sweet place for little ones to sit and watch the birds at your birdfeeder. If you don't have a little one to paint for, this little seat makes a great place for your favorite plant.

By Chris Stokes

SUPPLIES

Project Surface:

Child's chair

Acrylic craft paint:

For decorative painting the design

Apple Spice

Asphaltum

Burnt Umber

Buttercream

Ivory Black

Olive Green

Wicker White

Yellow Ochre

Paint Brushes:

Flat shaders - #8, #12

Round - #3

Rake or comb - 1/2"

Old toothbrush (for spattering)

Optional: Foam brush (for base painting)

Other Supplies:

Clear spray sealer, gloss sheen

Tracing paper and pencil

Transfer paper and stylus

Sandpaper

Tack cloth

INSTRUCTIONS

Prepare

1. Sand chair smooth. Wipe away dust.
2. *Option:* If your chair isn't painted or you want a creamy background color, paint chair with Buttercream. Let dry.
3. *Option:* Sand to create a distressed, worn look. Wipe away dust.
4. Trace and transfer pattern.

Paint the Design

Branches:

Using a #3 round multi-loaded with Asphaltum and Ivory Black/Yellow Ochre, wiggle limbs in.

House Finch:

1. Using a #3 round, tap in Apple Spice, Burnt Umber, Asphaltum, and Buttercream, blending as you paint.
2. Add details, using a liner loaded with inky Burnt Umber+ Ivory Black.
3. Highlight with Wicker White.
4. Paint eye with Burnt Umber. Paint pupil with Ivory Black. Add a Buttercream sparkle.
5. Paint the twigs in the bird's mouth with inky Burnt Umber + Yellow Ochre.

Background Leaves:

1. Multi-load a #8 flat shader with Yellow Ochre and Olive Green. Tip in Buttercream. Blend gently and wiggle in leaves.
2. Add details with inky Burnt Umber.

Nest & Eggs:

1. Using a 1/2" rake, pull inky lines of Burnt Umber/Asphaltum and Yellow Ochre to form the nest. Pick up Ivory Black for shaded area. Let dry.
2. Float in eggs with Burnt Umber and Buttercream. Highlight with Wicker White.
3. Using a liner, load inky Yellow Ochre and Wicker White. Pull messy twigs and grasses. Pull some Burnt Umber twigs here and there.
4. Shade with floated Asphaltum.

Flowers:

1. Using a #8 flat shader double loaded with Wicker White and Yellow Ochre, wiggle in each white petal. Flip some tips with floated Wicker White.
2. Paint red flower petals with Apple Spice and Buttercream.
3. Pounce centers with Burnt Umber and Olive Green.

Continued on page 117

Pattern for Chair Back
(actual size)

Pattern for Chair Seat

Enlarge @110% for actual size.

continued from page 115.

4. Highlight with Yellow Ochre + a touch of Wicker White.
5. Shade around centers with Asphaltum.
6. Add inky Burnt Umber and Wicker White pollen dots.

Foreground Leaves:
Multi-load a #12 flat shader with Burnt Umber, Olive Green, and Yellow Ochre. Tip in Buttercream. Paint leaves. Pick up a little Apple Spice for some. Let dry.

Finish

1. Spatter with inky Burnt Umber. Let dry.
2. Spray with gloss sealer. Let dry. ❏

MY LITTLE CHICKADEE LAMP

DECORATIVE PAINTING

Birds and berries are Chris's favorite things to paint. She found this simple ceramic lamp at a builder's supply company. You may have a similar lamp that you can give a new look with a painted design. She used cream-colored spray paint to warm the color of the white shade.

By Chris Stokes

SUPPLIES

Project Surface:

Ginger-jar style ceramic lamp with fabric shade

Acrylic craft paint:

For decorative painting piece

    Apple Spice

    Asphaltum

    Burnt Umber

    Ivory Black

    Olive Green

    Tapioca

Paint Brushes:

Flat shaders - #8, #12

Liner

Round - #3

Small stencil brush

Old scruffy brush *or* old stencil brush

Other Supplies:

Clear matte sealer spray

Clear satin sealer spray

Optional: Satin spray paint - Cream

Tracing paper and pencil

Transfer paper and stylus

Fine sandpaper

Paper towels

INSTRUCTIONS

Prepare

1. Wash ceramic lamp base gently with soap and water. Rinse well and dry.
2. Sand the design area lightly.
3. Spray with matte sealer. Let dry.
4. *Option:* Mist shade with cream spray paint. Let dry.
5. Trace and transfer patterns.

Paint the Lamp Base

Wreath:

1. Apply a light wash of Olive Green on the oval for wreath. Blot with a paper towel.
2. Using a scruffy brush or old stencil brush, dry brush the wreath area with Asphaltum and Olive Green. Let dry.
3. Using a liner brush, pull Asphaltum and Burnt Umber twigs to form wreath.
4. Lightly stroke in a few background inky leaves using the same colors.

Chickadee:

1. Using a #8 flat and a #3 round, tap in Tapioca + a touch of Yellow Ochre. Pick up Asphaltum and Burnt Umber to shade.
2. Highlight with Tapioca, using a liner for details.
3. Paint eyes with Burnt Umber. Paint pupil with Ivory Black. Highlight with a touch of Tapioca.

Berries:

1. Multi-load a small stencil brush with Apple Spice, Yellow Ochre, and touch of Tapioca. Twist in berries.
2. Pick up Burnt Umber to shade some berries.
3. Dot with Tapioca highlights.

Leaves:

1. Multi-load flat brushes with Olive Green and Burnt Umber to stroke leaves. Pick up Apple Spice and some Yellow Ochre.
2. Detail leaves, using a liner brush with inky Burnt Umber + Asphaltum.

Paint the Lamp Shade

Tip: Turn on the lamp so you can see the design as you work. If the paint is too thick it will look black when lighted—use very inky paint.

1. Wash the half circle with inky Olive Green.
2. Paint bows and trailing ribbons on corners, using a #3 round with inky Apple Spice.
3. Paint vines with inky Burnt Umber + Asphaltum.
4. Stroke leaves with inky Olive Green.

Continued on page 120

continued from page 118

5. Twist in berries, using a small stencil brush and inky Apple Spice. Shade, using the same color with more paint.

6. Detail some leaves with inky Burnt Umber.

7. Darken the right side of the ribbon with Apple Spice, using a liner brush. Let dry.

Finish

1. Paint bottom of lamp base with a wash of Apple Spice.

2. Paint middle ring of lamp base with a wash of Olive Green. Let dry.

3. Spatter lamp base and shade with inky Burnt Umber. Let dry.

4. Spray clear satin sealer on base. Let dry. ❏

Pattern for Shade
(actual size)

Section B

Connect Section A to Section B at
dotted lines to complete pattern.

Section A

LEAFY MOSAIC TABLES

PAINT AND MOSAIC TECHNIQUE

Kathi gave these table bases a rusty-looking sponged faux finish, and then she created two mosaic designs to replace the tables' plain glass tops. There are two different, coordinating designs for tops that use the same color tiles.

By Kathi Malarchuk Bailey

SUPPLIES

Project Surface:

2 metal table bases (They don't need to have glass.)

Hardboard pieces, sized to fit your tables

12" square ceramic tiles, sage green, tan, beige (purchase enough to cover the square footage of your table top)

Paints & Finishes:

Metal primer

Acrylic craft paint

   Black

   Dark Brown

   Rust

   Yellow Ochre

Matte sealer spray

Tools:

Foam brush

Wire cutters

Tile nippers

Hammer

Safety glasses

Rubber gloves

Bucket

Small trowel

Plastic scraper

Cellulose sponge (for grouting)

Cellulose sponges cut in small pieces

Other Supplies:

1 yd. copper wire

Waterproof adhesive

Tile grout

Newspapers *or* plastic sheeting

Sandpaper

Transfer paper and stylus

Tracing paper and pencil

Grout sealer

Disposable plate

INSTRUCTIONS

Prepare

1. Remove glass from table tops (if they had glass).
2. Sand edges of hardboard to smooth.
3. Trace patterns and transfer to rough sides of hardboard.
4. Use the patterns as guides to measure and cut copper wires for stems and veins.
5. To break tiles, place one on newspapers on a hard surface. Cover with additional newspapers. Wearing safety glasses, use a hammer to break the tile into small pieces. Repeat for each color tile. Store the pieces of each color separately.
6. Remove dust and grime from table bases.
7. Spray bases with two coats of metal primer. Let dry completely.

Create the Mosaics

1. Arrange the broken pieces of green tile on hardboard to fill in the leaves, breaking the tile pieces as needed to fit the pattern. Be sure to leave enough open space (1/4" to 3/8") in the vein and stem areas to place copper wire (where indicated) after grouting.

Continued on page 124

continued from page 122

2. Cut the wire for the stems and leaf veins. (**photo 2**)
3. Fill in the background with pieces of tan and beige tiles, breaking the tile pieces as needed with tile nippers. See the photographs for color placement.
4. Adhere tiles with waterproof glue. (**photo 1**) Allow to dry overnight.

Grout the Mosaics

1. Prepare grout in a disposable container according to manufacturer's instructions. We tinted our grout for the finished projects with Dark Brown and Black acrylic paint. When wet, the grout should be two times darker than the color you want it to be because the color will lighten as the grout dries.

Photo 1 - Gluing the tile pieces.

Photo 2 - Cutting wire for the veins using wire cutters.

Photo 3 - Applying grout.

2. Place panel on newspaper and/or plastic sheet. Use a trowel or old paintbrush to apply the grout. Use a plastic scraper or the brush to push grout around and down into the spaces **photo 3**), ensuring the entire area and sides are covered. Scrape or brush diagonally across entire surface to fill spaces.

3. Insert precut copper wires into stem and leaf vein areas. Be sure wire is placed at or slightly below the level of the tile. (**photo 4**) Wipe off excess grout that was pushed out by the wire. Allow to set approximately 15 minutes.

Photo 4 - Inserting a precut wire for a vein and stem.

4. Fill a bucket with clean water. Dampen sponge and start wiping off grout. Rinse sponge in bucket and replace water regularly. Continue until all of grout is removed from top of tiles. (A haze will appear on the tiles while drying.)

5. Continue to let dry, wiping off the haze with a clean, damp sponge until the tile is clear. Allow to dry thoroughly to cure.

6. Seal grout with grout sealer to prevent water damage. Let dry.

Sponge the Table Bases

1. Paint with two to three coats of Rust acrylic paint. Let dry between coats.

2. Pour small amounts of Black, Dark Brown, and Yellow Ochre on a disposable plate. Dampen small pieces of sponge. Dip a sponge in Dark Brown and lightly sponge over the basecoat, leaving some background showing.

3. Repeat with Black, then Yellow Ochre to achieve a mottled, rusty effect.

4. *Option:* Sponge some areas with Rust if enough of the background doesn't show through the Black and Dark Brown areas. Let dry.

Finish

1. Spray bases with matte sealer.
2. Insert mosaic tops in table bases. ❑

Pattern for Large Leaf
Enlarge @165% for actual size

Pattern for Small Leaf
Enlarge @ 200% for actual size.

METRIC CONVERSION CHART

Inches to Millimeters and Centimeters

Inches	MM	CM	Inches	MM	CM
1/8	3	.3	2	51	5.1
1/4	6	.6	3	76	7.6
3/8	10	1.0	4	102	10.2
1/2	13	1.3	5	127	12.7
5/8	16	1.6	6	152	15.2
3/4	19	1.9	7	178	17.8
7/8	22	2.2	8	203	20.3
1	25	2.5	9	229	22.9
1-1/4	32	3.2	10	254	25.4
1-1/2	38	3.8	11	279	27.9
1-3/4	44	4.4	12	305	30.5

Yards to Meters

Yards	Meters	Yards	Meters
1/8	.11	3	2.74
1/4	.23	4	3.66
3/8	.34	5	4.57
1/2	.46	6	5.49
5/8	.57	7	6.40
3/4	.69	8	7.32
7/8	.80	9	8.23
1	.91	10	9.14
2	1.83		

INDEX